RIVERSIDE RECIPES

RIVER
BOOKS

First published and distributed in 2014 by
River Books
396 Maharaj Road, Tatien, Bangkok 10200
Tel: (66 2) 622-1900, 622-1617 Fax: (66 2) 225-3861
E-mail: order@riverbooksbk.com
www.riverbooksbk.com

A River Books Production.

British Library Cataloguing-in-Publication Data.
A catalogue record for this book is available from the British Library.

ISBN 978-616-7339-36-8

Editor: Narisa Chakrabongse
Chef: Voravat Thonglor
Food Advisor: Montri Virojvejaphant
Photography: Kitti Bowornphatnon and Paisarn Piemmettawat
Food Stylist: Ekarin Yusuksomboon
Florist: Santhand Puangpitak
Production Supervision: Paisarn Piemmettawat
Design: Peerapong Pongprapapan, 1000 PONIES Co.,Ltd.

Printed in Thailand by Sirivatana Interprint Co., Ltd.

CONTENTS

INTRODUCTION

BY

NARISA CHAKRABONGSE

Chakrabongse House was built in 1908 as a private residence near the Grand Palace. Situated on the Chao Phraya River, it provided a place for Prince Chakrabongse to change before attending ceremonies in the palace or for him and his Russian wife, Ekaterina Desnitskaya (Katya), to relax and take boat trips on the river. The house was designed by Mario Tamagno, a Milanese architect who was also responsible for the Ministry of Commerce opposite Chakrabongse Villas. This latter building is now the Museum of Siam. The house is very much in the style of a bourgeois villa seen throughout Europe at the end of the nineteenth and early twentieth centuries. Particular features are the carved teak staircase, the high ceilings and the elegant double wooden doors which allowed air to flow from one room to another. At the top of the house a small shrine room houses Buddha images

QUEEN SAOWABHA BY MUI CHANTRALAKSHANA 1912

and portions of ashes from royal cremations. The glass enclosed structure is surrounded by a so-called widow's walk from where the viewer still has a panoramic view of the city, looking west to Khlong Bangkok Noi, Wat Kalaya, the Naval fort and Wat Arun, looking north to the Grand Palace, looking east to the Golden Mount and south towards the commercial district.

CHAKRABONGSE VILLAS

16

THE HOUSE IN 1938

Fortunately, the land, which is just behind the Temple of the Reclining Buddha and just north of the main fresh fruit and vegetable market, Pak Khlong Talad, was bought for the prince by his mother, Queen Saowabha, in a private capacity rather than forming part of the crown property. Thus in 1932 when the revolution changed the Absolute Monarchy into a Constitutional one, the house was owned by Prince Chula Chakrabongse, son of Katya and Chakrabongse, which prevented the Khana Rasadon from seizing the house. Paruskawan Palace was not so lucky and together with the residences of other high-ranking princes it was taken by the government and turned into a ministry.

At that time Prince Chula was at Cambridge reading history. Although he loved Chakrabongse House, as he called it, it never usurped the place in his heart of Paruskawan Palace, his childhood home. Indeed, he wrote in 1950 "I love Paruskawan, the house where I was born more than words can say and, though I have not passed a night within its friendly walls for

A CORNER OF THE SITTING ROOM WITH A PORTRAIT OF PRINCE CHULA AND HIS MOTHER, KATYA

PRINCE
CHAKRABONGSE
ON RAMUSHKA
IN THE UNIFORM
OF THE RUSSIAN
HUSSARS.

couple's divorce in 1919. The love story that had begun in the salons of St Petersburg and under the patronage of Tsar Nicholas II, did not have a happy ending after all.

THE RUSSIAN CONNECTION

When Nicholas II was the Tsarevitch he was sent on an Asian Tour between 1890 and 1891. In March 1891 he stayed in Bangkok as a guest of King Rama V and a firm friendship developed. As a result Nicholas told the king that he would look after the education of one of the king's sons and treat him as his own son. My grandfather, Prince Chakrabongse, second son of King Rama V and Queen Saowabha, was chosen. My grandfather first spent time in England, learning the language and Russian in preparation for his studies at the elite military academy, the Corps des Pages. The prince was an excellent student and spurred on by the competition of his fellow Thai, Nai Poum, he eventually graduated top of his class and became a Cornet in the Hussar regiment, where he even taught new recruits when officers were in short supply as a result of the Russo-Japanese war of 1905.

Prince Chakrabongse was indeed treated as a member of the Russian Imperial Family and attended many court functions. He lived in the Winter Palace, had the use of Imperial Carriages and was treated very much as one of the Tsar's family, being included in all important events and ceremonies. During his time at the Corps des Pages, he had been appointed as a Kammer page to Empress Alexandra and in that capacity attended grand balls and state events.

As with high-class Russians of the day, Prince Chakrabongse often attended the ballet and even had a flirtation with Kschessinskaya, a prima ballerina who had been a mistress of the Tsar and later was linked with two grand dukes. However it was in 1905 that he met the Russian woman who would change his life.

Katya and my grandfather had met in the salon of a widow named Mme Chrapovitzkaya in St Petersburg. As the Russo-Japanese war had just begun, Katya was

many years, it is the only place really meaning home to me."

Despite being brought up in a palace with a large garden and being much loved by his grandmother Queen Saowabha, my father's childhood ended abruptly in 1920 when he was just 12. In the autumn of 1919 his grandmother had died aged only 58 and she was followed shortly after by Chula's father in June 1920. Only 37 at the time, his son and his new young and beautiful wife, Princess Chavalit Obhas, were at his side in Singapore. My father's grief must have been augmented by a difficult situation in which on his deathbed, my grandfather had scrawled a new will leaving all his possessions and property to his new wife. It was his affair with the princess while his wife, Katya, was taking a trip to Japan in 1918 that had led to the

18

it seems extraordinary to me that he dared not only to challenge his father but also to leave Russia without saying goodbye to his patron Tsar Nicholas II.

PRINCE CHULA: THE ENGLISH CONNECTION

Upon the death of his father, Prince Chula now came under the guardianship of King Vajiravudh, Rama VI, who, childless until the day he died, loved his nephew greatly. Overturning the will, he decreed that Princess Chaovalit could enjoy the properties while she was alive but that ultimately they belonged to my father.

While my father was in England, his uncle and guardian the king died in November 1925, aged only 45, and with that he lost a much-loved father figure. King Prajadhipok, the youngest of Queen Saowabha's five sons with King Chulalongkorn, now acceded to the throne and became my

preparing to go to the front as a nurse. Their relationship was tested by months of enforced separation and there must have PHOTOGRAPHS OF PRINCE CHAKRABONGSE, KATYA AND PRINCE CHULA

been great uncertainty on both sides. Katya, who was born and grew up in Kiev in the Ukraine, had become an orphan at 16 and although she had a brother who also lived in St Petersburg, she seems to have been very much alone in the world, her half-sister and brother from her mother's remarriage being more of a burden than a support. Faced with an uncertain future in a Russia that was increasingly politically unstable after the revolution of 1905, marriage to a charismatic Siamese prince must have seemed exciting and a way out.

After some prevarication, in the spring of 1906, Prince Chakrabongse and Katya eloped to Constantinople to get married in a Greek Orthodox church, spent a honeymoon in Cairo and a few months in Singapore, before King Chulalongkorn found out about the secret marriage. A marriage outside the family to a foreigner had never happened before. Indeed, the Thai tradition was to marry close relatives, thereby concentrating power in the centre. As the king was considered to be semi-divine, it was also thought to be wrong for a royal prince to marry a foreign commoner.

Reading my grandfather's letters to his father only a few months before this hazardous elopement,

PRINCE CHULA AND LISBA

19

father's guardian. Their relationship was not so cordial and among other things, King Prajadhipok warned his nephew not to repeat the wrongs of his father by marrying a foreigner. Although my father may have tried to follow this instruction, living in the UK for such a long time brought him into contact with many English girls and eventually he was introduced to my future mother, Elisabeth Hunter, through my father's cousin Prince Bira. At the time the two were running a successful motor racing equipe called the White Mouse team and through their wins at Monaco, Crystal Palace, Donington, Brooklands and elsewhere had brought the Thai flag and the Thai national anthem to the attention of British and European race goers.

Despite trying to resist my mother for a while, Prince Chula succumbed and they were married in 1938 on the day that Neville Chamberlain proclaimed that he had secured 'Peace in our time', 30th September. Prince Bira had also recently got married and in 1938 the two couples came to Thailand by sea. It was the first time that my mother had seen her new Bangkok home. Although the trip was a success, the Second World War put paid to any plans my father and mother might have had to make Bangkok a more permanent home. On the outbreak of war, my father decided that they should move to Cornwall to avoid potential bombing and after the Japanese invasion in December 1941 and Thailand's declaration of war against the UK, he and my mother were technically enemy aliens. However, through his connections in the government they were allowed to stay and my father even joined the Home Guard, something of which he was very proud.

I think this break from Thailand meant that for the rest of their lives, my parents were to view Chakrabongse House very much as a second home and the house always had a slightly unloved air. Interior decoration hurriedly carried out before their pre-war trip remained unchanged, and Thai antiques and artefacts, which could have been used in the rooms, languished in the cellar.

THE WRITER, AGED 3,
WITH CHULA
AND LISBA ARRIVING
AT HUA LAMPHONG

ANGLO-RUSSIAN-THAI: CHAKRABONGSE HOUSE BECOMES A HOME

After my father's death in December 1963, my mother and I still came to Thailand and true to her promise to my father that I would be bilingual, she insisted that I spend one term a year at Chitralada School within the grounds of the palace where King Rama IX and his family resided. Although this schooling was very difficult at the time, it did ensure that I learned to speak, read and write Thai fluently, something which has proved invaluable ever since.

Then in 1971 my mother died and the house became even sadder. I spent the next 12 years or so studying and then getting married, beginning a life which seemed very London-based. However, things often don't go according to plan and by 1984, I was in Bangkok and living in Chakrabongse House.

Many people suggested that it must be scary living in an old house (Thais are firm believers in ghosts) full of dark teak and family portraits, but for me it felt totally comfortable. I finally understood that unlike my grandfather for whom the house had been simply a useful place to get changed for palace ceremonies, or my father for whom the house was always a poor substitute for Paruskawan Palace, this really was my home.

Gradually I began rooting around in the cellar, unpacking boxes of Benjarong multi-coloured porcelain and old stereoscope slides, scouring antique shops for old mirrors, and shipping family portraits back from England. I enclosed the terrace on the riverside, which had been noisy, hot and full of mosquitoes when I was a child, to create a winter garden room where the family could relax and live informally. I also installed a Western-style kitchen so I could cook simple meals myself. I rearranged my father's books (he was a well-known writer and historian in Thailand) and researched my grandfather's letters and diaries. I got fully involved in creating my publishing company, River Books, producing books on Southeast Asian art, culture and history and met hundreds of relatives whom I had never seen before.

As time passed, however, I could see that the house had structural problems that needed urgent attention. The wiring in the house had not been looked at for almost 90 years and was definitely a fire hazard. The plumbing was also in a dire state, the roof needed replacing and the whole house needed repainting. I engaged an excellent firm who had renovated several old villas and palaces but the work took a long time and a lot of money. I wondered how I could finance the renovation and ensure that the property stayed looking good, while I was living part of the year in England.

Together with my half-Thai, half-English husband, Gee Svasti Thomson, we thought that creating some luxury suites in the garden could be a solution. At the time, boutique hotels were very much of a rarity in Bangkok and I felt certain that the beauty of the location in the heart of old Bangkok and looking across to the iconic Temple of the Dawn would give visitors to Bangkok something really special.

By this time, I had, together with Khun Paisarn Piemmettawat, been running River Books for around 10 years. Creating a small hotel seemed to be something that would be more fun and relaxing than the stress of editing (we had just finished the Oxford-River Books English-Thai dictionary) and publishing. Anyone who has ever been involved in the hospitality business will laugh at this point and soon the rose-tinted spectacles came off, but nevertheless I think transforming the house and grounds in the way we have and not selfishly keeping the beauty of the site just for me and my family has been a good decision.

BETEL NUT SET

21

A CORNER OF
THE GREEN ROOM

CHAKRABONGSE DINING

At first the hotel catered only for in-house guests, but gradually with the food improving steadily, more and more people begged to be allowed to come and dine by the Chao Phraya River, to enjoy classic Thai food or innovative dishes from a frequently-changing daily menu.

Several years after opening the dining room to outside guests, we have decided to produce a cookbook to share our food with our friends and guests.

ROOTS OF THAI CUISINE

Today Thai restaurants are ubiquitous throughout the world and regularly come near the top in surveys of the world's favourite cuisines. The rise of Thai food in the international arena has been swift. When I first came to London in 1972 there was only one or two Thai restaurants compared with the hundreds found today with over 2,000 in the UK as a whole. In the list of the "World's 50 most delicious foods", compiled by CNN in 2011, *som tum* (unripe papaya salad) came 46th, *nam tok mu* (spicy grilled pork) 19th, *tom yum kung* (spicy and sour prawn soup) was 8th, and Massaman curry (a Muslim-derived curry) took first place as the most delicious food in the world.

Such lists are somewhat trivial but the dishes featured reflect the fact that Thai cuisine derives from a rich mix of influences, accumulated and transformed over many centuries. Situated between two major civilisations — India to the west and China to the east — the history of Siam, present-day Thailand, is equally complex. Archaeological finds in Southern Thailand attest to its importance as an entrepot on the maritime trade route between Europe, India and China before the first millenia CE, while by the 16th century, Ayutthaya, the ancient capital further up the Chao Phraya River, was one of the most important trading centres of Southeast Asia, welcoming merchants from all over the world. Among these the Portuguese were the first to have diplomatic relations with Siam in 1543 and from the Portuguese came the chilli, which in turn had come from South America. In addition, Portuguese seafarers introduced the egg-based sweets, which were adapted into the *foi thong* and *thong yib*.

Thailand's more immediate neighbours have also played an important role, exerting influences, which are reflected in the country's regional culinary diversity. Thus Northern Thai (Lanna) cuisine betrays Burmese influences as it was part of the Burmese kingdom for over 200 years; Southern Thai cuisine owes much to its Muslim neighbour Malaysia; and the Northeast (Isaan), although technically part of Siam from the late 18th century, remained very independent until the latter part of the 19th century, an independence reflected in its cuisine. Not only do the curries and soups reflect diverse roots, but so too the rice, with the North and Northeast preferring sticky rice to the more fragrant long-grained rice of the Central plain.

It is the central region which is perhaps most emblematic of what is perceived as a classic Thai meal — jasmine rice accompanied by four or five dishes comprising a curry such as green *kaeng khiew wan* or red *Massaman*; a fish dish,

SOME OF MY FATHER'S BOOKS.

22

whether a freshwater catfish or a sea fish such as sea bass; a soup such as *tom kha gai* based around galangal and coconut milk or the famous *tom yum* with spicy and sour notes; stir fried vegetables; a spicy salad, *yum*, which are diverse and delicious and perhaps another stir fry. Meals are generally a social activity with friends or family passing dishes around and everyone taking a couple of spoonfuls at a time rather than piling everything on the plate in one go. Thais eat with a spoon and fork except for dishes with sticky rice where the fingers are traditionally used or noodle dishes, which are eaten with chopsticks. Such noodle dishes are often eaten at lunchtime when Thais generally favour a one-plate dish such as *phad Thai*, *khao phad*, or *kai yang som tum*. Often these are sold at street stalls specialising

in a particular delicacy. Seasonings comprise a mix of hot, sour, salty and sweet that make Thai food so delectable. As David Thompson, the Australian chef of Nahm fame, has said: "Thai food ain't about simplicity. It's about the juggling of disparate elements to create a harmonious finish. Like a complex musical chord it's got to have a smooth surface but it doesn't matter what's happening underneath. Simplicity isn't the dictum here, at all. Some westerners think it's a jumble of flavours, but to a Thai that's important, it's the complexity they delight in."

I first encountered Thai food in a conscious way at my Thai day school where I went between the ages of seven to eleven for one term a year. The whole experience was somewhat traumatic as studying for one term instead of three, I was always struggling to keep up apart from in English where I came top of the class, unsurprisingly, and maths which at primary level was essentially the same. Lunchtime was a bit of an ordeal as I struggled with unfamiliar foods and tastes. *Kaeng leuang*, yellow curry with bamboo shoots, was particularly difficult but I loved the sweets of set coconut cream and jelly or golden threads. At home in Chakrabongse House, like all Thai children I loved to eat fried rice and *kai sateh*, often challenging my uncle to see who could eat the most and once managing 30 sticks in one go. Later after my mother died I was occasionally invited to Sukhothai Palace where the dowager Queen Rambhai lived. The first time I went I was horrified when after tucking into a full English meal at dinner, I realized there was a complete Thai menu still to come. In fact, this was common practice in royal palaces and in my grandfather's home, Paruskawan Palace, there was not only a Thai chef but a Russian one as well, who once got so drunk he fell in the canal. However, it was only when I came back to Thailand in 1984 that my initiation into Thai cuisine truly began.

23

As well as teaching English at my old school Chitralada, I undertook some work as an interpreter and translator for the Thai army in connection with their development work for Thai villages

DINNER BY
THE RIVER.

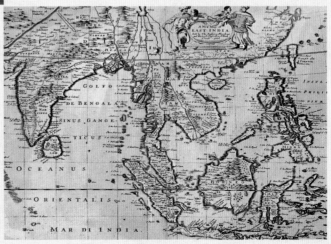

affected by the influx of refugees all around the border and the establishment of refugee camps where the inmates often had better food and healthcare than the local villagers. As a result I got to travel the length and breadth of the country, staying in army camps, eating in petrol stations and sitting down with the locals. While conversations invariably started with the words: *"Taan phed dai reua plao? Can you eat spicy food?"*, they soon realised I loved trying new things.

At Chakrabongse Villas, the menus are predominantly central Thai but with a fresh twist and an emphasis on healthy recipes. We don't use pork, despite the fact that it is often ubiquitous elsewhere even on allegedly vegetarian dishes, and use low-sodium fish sauce and soy sauce as well as organic, hand-milled rice. The vegetables and fruit come from Pak Khlong Talad and the fish and meat from Klong Toey markets. Because of our policy of working around a daily menu, there is little waste and everything is totally fresh.

We hope you will enjoy these recipes from the Chakrabongse Villas kitchen under the control of Chef Wat and that they will help you create well-balanced tasty Thai meals.

A DAY IN A LIFE OF EATING THAI FOOD

Breakfast in the Western understanding of the term is not very Thai. At Chakrabongse Villas, guests can enjoy a full English Breakfast, or try rice soup or rice porridge. Nowadays many Thais probably eat a continental breakfast, grabbed on the way to work, but generally breakfast in Thailand is much more likely to be a rice soup with fish, chicken or prawns, or a plate of fried rice. When I was small my special treat was *pla tongo* with condensed milk — a sort of deep fried Thai croissant — or *khanom krok*, small coconut custards cooked in a special earthen ware dish over charcoal.

Lunch is often just a single dish — *ahaan jaan diew* — based either around rice or noodles. The famous fried rice is perennially popular as is rice with *kapraw* and chicken, prawn or pork, while *kuae tiew* (noodles) in all the varieties, whether wide, thin, glass or egg noodles,

reflect the important strand of Chinese influence in Thai cuisine. Chinese from the South, mainly Guangdong, began emigrating to Thailand in large numbers in the the mid-19th century, although there have been Chinese in Thailand for over 400 years and Thai-Chinese trade was the foundation for Thai

24

wealth in the 18ᵗʰ and 19ᵗʰ centuries. Today, Thailand has the largest and best-integrated overseas Chinese community in the world with Thais of Chinese ethnicity numbering around nine million people, or 14% of the Thai population. Chinese-derived lunch-time recipes include *kuae tiew* and *khanom chin*.

Although in the past, Thai food was not designed to be eaten at cocktail functions, a Western concept, many dishes adapt well and a selection such as *miang kum, ma ho, muu sateh,* are included in the book. Others such as *tod mun pla krai* or chicken sateh are also suitable.

In the evening comes the classic Thai dinner which at Chakrabongse Villas is served in the beautiful riverside sala. The trick to creating a perfect Thai meal is a harmonious combination of flavours and textures — one curry, a crispy salad dish, a palate-calming vegetable dish, a soup and a stir fry, all served with rice — followed by classic Thai desserts, which are often based around coconut and palm sugar.

All recipes are arranged for four people.

25

BREAKFAST

RICE PORRIDGE WITH SALTED EGG AND MINCED CHICKEN

Khao tom khai kem nueng kai sub

Ingredients
2 cups brown rice
3 leaves fresh pandanus
2½ litres water

Place rice and water in a saucepan and set on the stove. Add the pandanus leaves tied in a knot. Boil until cooked and the rice grains have swollen as desired with a fragrant smell. Stir frequently to prevent sticking to the bottom and burning.

Ingredients for steamed salted egg and minced chicken
200 grams minced chicken
3 salted egg yolks
2 tablespoons pounded coriander root,
   garlic and peppercorns
1 egg white
2 teaspoons castor sugar
1 teaspoon salt
3 tablespoons flour [paeng mun]
½ teaspoon sesame oil

1. In a bowl mix together the minced chicken, coriander root, garlic, peppercorns, white egg, sugar, salt and 2 tablespoons of flour. Knead until it is sticky.
2. Divide the mixture into balls of about 20 grams each and make an indentation in the middle. Arrange in a deep dish.
3. Form the salted egg yolks into small balls and place in the hollows of the chicken pieces.
4. Prepare the steamer and when the water underneath is boiling, place the dish in the top part and steam until cooked.
5. Take the water surrounding the chicken balls and bring to a boil in a pan. Add a little water to the remaining tablespoon of flour and mix well. This will thicken into a sauce, which can be dribbled over the steamed chicken. Eat with the boiled brown rice.

CRISPY PRAWN SALAD WITH YOUNG GINGER

Yum kung krob khing on

This is served as an accompaniment to rice soup.

Ingredients

100 grams dried crispy prawns
2 red shallots
2 spring onions
3 red bird's eye chillies
1 knob ginger
2 tablespoons lime juice
1 tablespoon fish sauce
1 tablespoon castor sugar
½ litre vegetable oil for frying

1. Wash the crispy prawns. Soak briefly then drain water and fry the prawns until golden.
2. Peel and wash the shallots and slice finely. Chop the spring onion and bird's eye chillies into fine roundels. Peel the ginger and slice thinly, then cut into fine strips. Set aside.
3. Mix the lime juice, fish sauce and sugar thoroughly. Add the other chopped ingredients together with the fried prawns and toss till well mixed. Serve in a bowl as an accompaniment to boiled rice soup.

35

RICE PORRIDGE WITH CHICKEN, MUSHROOMS AND EGG
Khao tom kai hed hom khai luok

Ingredients
1 cup jasmine rice
1½ litres water
2 pandanus leaves
1 chicken breast
3 tablespoons salt

1. Rinse the rice and place in a large pan. Tie the pandanus leaves into a knot and add to the rice. Add 1½ litres of water. Bring to a boil and continue simmering, stirring from time to time to prevent the rice grains sticking to the bottom. When properly cooked, remove from the heat and set aside.
2. Place the chicken breast in a pan, cover with water and bring to a boil. Add 3 tablespoons of salt. Reduce to a simmer. When cooked, remove, allow to cool before tearing into shreds to be served with *khao tom*.

FRIED SHITAKE MUSHROOMS
Ingredients
100 grams fresh shitake mushrooms
1 tablespoon chopped garlic
1 tablespoon white soy sauce
1 teaspoon ground black pepper
½ teaspoon sugar
1 tablespoon vegetable oil

1. Wash the the mushrooms and remove the stalks. Slice thinly.
2. Pound the garlic to crush, then chop roughly. Heat the oil in a wok and fry the garlic until fragrant.
3. Add the mushrooms. Season to taste with white soy sauce, sugar and pepper. Fry till the mushrooms are cooked.

BOILED EGG
Softly boil an egg for 2-3 minutes.

CRISPY PLA TONG KO
Ingredients
1 cup plain flour
1 tablespoon baking powder
1 teaspoon sugar
½ teaspoon salt
½ cup limewater
½ litre vegetable oil

1. Mix the flour, baking powder, sugar, salt and limewater in a bowl.
2. Knead until the ingredients are well mixed. Rest the pastry for 20 minutes before rolling out into a 1½ cm.
3. Cut the pastry into long strips about ½ cm wide. Cut these into 4 cm lengths.
4. Heat the oil in a pan and fry the pieces of pastry until crisp and golden.

36

FRIED JUTE LEAVES WITH DRIED SCALLOPS
Pad bai po hoy shell

Another ingredient for eating with rice porridge.

Ingredients
100 grams jute leaves
2 blocks dried scallops
2 tablespoons chopped garlic
2 litres water
2 tablespoons vegetable oil
2 teaspoons sugar
1 teaspoon ground black pepper

1. Boil the dried scallops in 1 litre of water. As soon as the water has come to a boil, reduce heat and simmer until they are soft. Drain the water and tear the scallops into strips.
2. Briefly blanch the jute leaves and rinse in fresh water to reduce their saltiness.
3. Heat the oil in a wok and fry the chopped garlic. Once it is fragrant add the jute leaves and the scallops. Season to taste with sugar and ground pepper. Serve as an accompaniment to the rice porridge.

39

RICE PORRIDGE WITH SEA BASS
Khao tom pla kapong

Khao tom of various kinds is a very popular dish with Thais. As with many of these types of dishes, dried chilli, chilli in vinegar, extra fish sauce and sugar are added according to individual taste. Prawns, fish or pork can be substituted for the chicken.

Ingredients
100 grams Jasmine rice
½ litre water
1 sea bass
1 teaspoon salt
2 tablespoons white soya sauce
1 teaspoon ground black pepper
4 cups of chicken stock
2 spring onions, chopped
1 bunch coriander
2 tablespoons fried garlic
2 tablespoons finely shredded ginger

1. Boil the Jasmine rice with the water to make a thick porridge.
2. Debone and slice the sea bass into pieces approximately 1 x 2 inches. Wash thoroughly. Bring two cups of chicken stock to a boil. Add ½ a tablespoon of shredded ginger, 1 teaspoon of salt, followed by the sliced sea bass. Do not stir. The fish will be cooked after 3-5 minutes. Take off the heat. Mix thoroughly and use your hand to throw the mixture into the bowl several times so it becomes sticky.
3. Take 2 more cups of stock in a pan and bring to a boil and simmer for 5-10 minutes. Spoon the cooked rice into the stock and season to taste with 1 teaspoon of salt, 2 tablespoons of white soya sauce. Ladle into a bowl.
4. Spoon the cooked fish onto the rice porridge and sprinkle with shredded ginger, spring onions, coriander, fried garlic and ground black pepper. Serve together with tao jiew sauce.

40

Ingredients for chicken stock
200 grams chicken bones
½ litre water

Wash the chicken bones, then place in a saucepan with the water. Bring to a boil for 5 minutes, skimming off any froth which forms. Then lower the heat and simmer for a further 30 minutes. Strain and keep just the stock.

Ingredients for fried garlic
100 grams garlic
300 mililitres vegetable oil

Finely chop the garlic. Heat the oil in a pan over a medium heat. After 2 minutes add the garlic and keep stirring to ensure even cooking for about 5 minutes. When the garlic begins to cook it will float to the surface. When the garlic turns golden remove with a slotted spoon and dry on kitchen paper.

Ingredients for fermented soya sauce (*tao jiew*)
2 tablespoons bird's eye chillies
2 tablespoons garlic
2 tablespoons fermented soya
2 tablespoons lime
2 teaspoons fish sauce
1 teaspoon castor sugar

Finely pound together the chillies and garlic. Add the fermented soya and pound lightly to mix. Add the fish sauce, castor sugar and lime juice, mixing well. The sauce should have the three tastes of sour, salty and sweet.

COCONUT CUSTARD CUPCAKES
Khanom krok

These tasty mouthfuls of coconut delight are a favourite with all Thai children and are best eaten hot. They are traditionally made in a metal or terracotta mould over a charcoal brazier. Various ingredients can be added to the topping mixture such as sweetcorn or taro.

Cupcake Ingredients
1½ cups rice flour
1 cup cooked rice
1 cup grated white coconut
1 egg yolk
½ cup castor sugar
1½ cups coconut cream
1 cup of limewater
1 teaspoon salt
1 cup vegetable oil
2 spring onions, finely sliced

Filling Ingredients
1 cup coconut cream
½ cup castor sugar
1 teaspoon salt

1. Mix the cooked rice, grated coconut, egg yolk, sugar, coconut cream and limewater in a food processor. After this sieve through a fine white cloth to remove the liquid and add the rice flour. Mix well and rest.
2. Mix together the coconut cream, castor sugar and salt. Pour into a saucepan. Stir while bringing to a boil. Don't let the coconut cream separate.
3. Place the *khanom krok* mould on the stove over a low heat. When making the cups, wipe the moulds with vegetable or coconut cream first.
4. Pour the mixture into the mould but don't fill it. Then pour on the topping. Cover with a lid. When they are cooked (about 3-5 minutes), remove them from the mould with a teaspoon and lay on a plate.

43

LUSCIOUS LUNCH

Chakraben

Ingredients

20 dried fried bird's eye chillies
I cup roasted shallots
I cup roasted garlic
2 tablespoons dry fried galangal
2 cups fried garlic
2 cups fried onion
I tablespoon roasted shrimp paste
3 tablespoons salt
I½ cups mung beans (skins removed) soaked
I½ cups fried peanuts
2 cups cooked prawns
I cup castor sugar
I cup palm sugar
I cup tamarind water
I½ cup citrus juice
I cup Kaffir lime juice
6 cups coconut cream
2 pieces halved Kaffir lime
2 litres vegetable oil

I. Take I tablespoon salt, roasted galangal, roasted shallot and roasted garlic and pound finely in a mortar. Add the fried chillies, fried onion, fried garlic and pound thoroughly. Add the roasted shrimp paste and pound again. Set aside.

2. Take the soaked beans and pound thoroughly. Set aside. Pound the fried peanuts but not too finely. Set aside. Roughly pound the boiled prawns.

3. Pour 2 cups coconut cream into a pan and heat until it separates. Add the pulverised spices and cook till fragrant. Add the crushed beans and then the peanuts, followed by the minced prawns. Add the remaining coconut cream. Season to taste with the castor sugar, palm sugar, salt, tamarind water, Kaffir lime juice and citrus juice (*Citrus medica*). Add the halved Kaffir lime. When the taste is correct, remove from the heat and set aside.

CHINESE RICE NOODLES WITH BEAN CURRY SAUCE

Khanom chin nam prik

NOODLES

In Thailand we buy our noodles ready made in the market. You can substitute dried Vietnamese noodles, twist them into portion-sized balls and arrange on a serving dish.

FRIED VEGETABLES

Morning glory leaves, various Thai edible flowers. Dip the flowers and leaves in batter and fry in batches.

FRESH VEGETABLES

Snake beans, banana flower, *kratin* tips (lead tree). Slice the snake beans finely. Take the tender part of the banana flower, slice finely and soak in lime juice.

BOILED VEGETABLES

Winged beans. Boil then refresh in iced water. Slice quite finely.

BOILED EGGS

Hard boil the eggs for IO minutes. Cool in cold water. Peel and slice just before serving.

FRIED PRAWNS AND CHILLIES

Peel and clean the tiger prawns. Stretch them out straight. Dip in batter and fry fill crisp and golden. Fry the dried bird's eye chillies until crisp. Arrange all the ingredients on a dish around the noodle balls and serve with the *nam prik* sauce.

51

FRIED RICE
WITH SEA BASS
Khao phad khai tom pla tod

Ingredients
2 cups cooked rice
2 hard-boiled eggs
150 grams sea bass fillet, diced
¼ cup vegetable oil to fry the rice
2 teaspoons white soy sauce
I tablespoon sugar
I teaspoon salt
I teaspoon ground black pepper
2 tablespoons batter flour
½ litre oil for frying fish

1. Hard boil the egg. When cool, peel and cut into cubes.
2. Take the diced sea bass fillet and marinade in the soy sauce before lightly coating with batter flour and frying in hot oil until cooked.
3. Add vegetable oil to the wok and when hot add the cooked rice. Flavour with white soya sauce, salt, sugar and ground black pepper. Add the fried sea bass and mix well. Finally add the hard-boiled eggs and toss gently. Spoon into a serving dish.

52

PHAD THAI WITH PRAWNS WRAPPED IN OMELETTE

Phad Thai sen jun mun kung ho khai

Ingredients

10 tiger prawns
200 grams Chantaburi noodles
¼ cup prawn roe
5 hens' eggs
3 red shallots
300 grams beansprouts
100 grams *kui chai* – Chinese leek
1 slice tofu
¼ cup dried shrimp
¼ cup chopped, sweet dried radish
¼ cup roasted chopped peanuts
½ cup tamarind water
½ cup palm sugar
½ cup fish sauce
1 cup water
½ litre vegetable oil

1. Peel the prawns and remove black strip from their backs. Peel the red shallots and slice finely. Wash the beansprouts and Chinese leek, cutting the latter in half. Use the lower part as an accompaniment and the top dark green part in the phad Thai chopped into 1 inch lengths. Chop the yellow tofu into small pieces. Wash the dried shrimp. Wash the sweet dried radish and slice finely.

2. Preparing the phad Thai sauce: Heat the oil in the wok. When hot add the shallots and cook till fragrant, add the tamarind water, fish sauce and sugar. Stir till the sugar dissolves and cook until sticky then set aside.

3. Beat three eggs. Fry in the pan to make two very thin omelettes. Remove and set aside. Heat the remaining oil and when hot fry the yellow tofu and the dried shrimp, chopped dried radish and the tiger prawns. When they are well mixed, crack the two remaining eggs into the pan. Stir well. When the eggs begin to cook, add the noodles. Mix well together and add some water. Toss them until they are soft and then add the phad Thai sauce prepared earlier together with the prawn fat.

4. Mix in half the beansprouts and the chopped Chinese leek tops followed by the chopped peanuts. Stir so that everything is well mixed. Remove from the heat.

5. Place the thin omelette on a serving dish. Spoon the phad Thai on top and fold the omelette around it. Arrange the accompaniments: the bean sprouts, Chinese leek stems, the finely chopped banana flower, segmented lime and roasted chilli flakes before serving.

55

FRIED RICE WITH GREEN CURRY PASTE

Khao phad prik kaeng khiew wan

Ingredients
2 cups cooked rice
150 grams chicken breast
¼ cup green curry paste
2 cups coconut cream
5 small green aubergines
½ cup pea aubergines
1 red finger chilli
50 grams holy basil
3 tablespoons fish sauce
4 tablespoons sugar

1. Wash and clean the chicken and vegetables and cut into bite-sized pieces. Marinade in ¼ cup coconut cream. Season to taste with fish sauce and sugar and set aside. Remove the stems of the round aubergines and segment into bite-sized pieces. Slice the finger chilli diagonally. Pluck the holy basil into individual leaves.

2. Heat 1 cup coconut cream until it separates. Add the spices and fry until fragrant. Add the marinaded chicken and cook till done. Add the chopped round aubergines, the pea aubergines, the red chilli and season to taste with fish sauce and sugar. Add the rice and mix thoroughly. Add half the holy basil and stir thoroughly. Remove from the heat and spoon into a serving dish.

CURRY PASTE
Ingredients
15 green finger chillies
10 red bird's eye chillies
1 tablespoon coriander root
¼ cup sliced red shallots
¼ cup garlic
1 tablespoon galangal sliced in roundels
3 tablespoons lemongrass finely sliced
1 teaspoon Kaffir lime zest
1 teaspoon peppercorns
1 teaspoon roasted coriander seed
1 teaspoon roasted cumin
1 teaspoon salt
1 teaspoon shrimp paste

For method see pages 188-189.

Accompaniments
Chinese-style chicken sausage fried at medium heat until cooked. Slice the *pla salid*. Fillet and fry until golden and crispy salted egg. Peel and slice finely holy basil. Fry in oil until crispy and use as garnish.

56

CLEAR SOUP WITH ROAST DUCK AND SWEET BASIL

Kaeng jeud ped yang bai horapa

Ingredients
8 cups water
1 roast duck
50 grams sweet basil
100 grams galangal
100 grams lemongrass
100 grams red shallots
50 grams garlic
5 Kaffir lime leaves
½ cup lime juice
½ cup fish sauce
½ cup castor sugar
4 coriander roots
4 dried fried bird's eye chillies

1. Remove the meat from the pre-roasted duck. Set aside the duck bones for the soup broth.
2. Crush the galangal and chop coarsely. Crush the lemongrass and cut into small sticks. Tear the Kaffir lime leaves. Pound the chillies just enough to split open. Wash the coriander roots and peel, crush and halve the shallots. Peel the garlic.
3. Boil the water and add the duck bones, the lemongrass, galangal, red shallots, garlic, Kaffir lime leaves, coriander root and dried chillies. Simmer until fragrant (about ½ hour).
4. Season to taste with sugar and fish sauce. Continue simmering until liquid has reduced to about 5 cups. Add the lime juice. Taste and check that it has the three flavours of sweet, salty and sour.
5. Slice the duck into thin pieces and set aside. Pluck off some basil leaves and line the soup bowls with them. Then add a layer of duck and pour on just the liquid from the soup to cover the duck. Sprinkle with chopped dried chilli before serving.

59

Ingredients

150 grams unripe papaya
40 grams carrot
40 grams long green beans
40 grams cherry tomatoes
8 bird's eye chillies
6 cloves garlic
2 tablespoons dried shrimps
¼ cup fish sauce
¼ cup palm sugar
¼ cup tamarind water
2 limes
¼ cup roasted peanuts

1. Place the fish sauce, palm sugar and tamarind water in a pan and heat until the sugar dissolves. Set aside. Peel the papaya and grate into strips. You can use a julienne peeler for this. Wash and chop the green beans into sticks. Halve the cherry tomatoes. Peel carrots and use julienne peeler to make strips.
2. Pound the chilli and garlic. Then add the dried shrimp, tomatoes and green beans and pound lightly to crush. Pour over the sauce, followed by the strips of unripe papaya, carrot and the roasted peanuts. Pound gently. Mix thoroughly. Check seasoning and serve.

GRILLED CHICKEN
Ingredients

2 chicken thighs
2 tablespoons coriander root
1 tablespoon garlic
1 tablespoon lemongrass
1 tablespoon ground turmeric
1 tablespoon white soya
1 tablespoon sugar
1 tablespoon fish sauce
1 tablespoon peppercorns

Take two chicken thighs, remove the meat and cut into two pieces. Pound together the coriander root, garlic, peppercorns, lemongrass and cumin.

SOM TUM THAI, GRILLED CHICKEN AND STICKY RICE
Som Tum Thai kai yang khao niew nueng

Use to marinade chicken for 20 mins. Season to taste with 1 tablespoon white soya sauce, 1 tablespoon sugar and 1 teaspoon fish sauce. Grill over charcoal on medium heat until cooked. Cut into bite-sized pieces.

BLACK STICKY RICE
Ingredients

250 grams black sticky rice
250 grams white sticky rice
2 litres water

1. Take the black and white sticky rice and rinse together, then soak in the 2 litres of water overnight.
2. Put the water in a steamer and bring to boil. Prepare a white cloth to support the top part.
3. Pour away the water in which rice has been soaking and rinse the rice briefly. Pour the rice onto the muslin which is lining the top part. Place on the steamer. Close the lid and bring water to a boil. Cook till the rice is done (approximately 25 minutes).
4. Stir the rice with a spoon or wooden paddle to release the heat and transfer to a dish before serving.

There are several variants of som tum. Som Tum Thai is the classic version and has peanuts, whereas the others do not.

60

SPICY CATFISH SALAD
Laab pla duk

This dish is typical of Isaan food and one of my favourites.
If catfish is not available mackerel could be substituted.
The key is to fry the fish until it is crispy.

Ingredients

2 catfish filleted

3 red shallots

2 spring onions

1 bunch saw-leaf coriander

2 Kaffir lime leaves

20 grams mint

1 tablespoon dried, roasted and milled chilli

2 tablespoons roasted milled rice

1 tablespoon fish sauce

½ tablespoon lime juice

1 litre vegetable oil

1. Cut the catfish fillets into bite-sized pieces. Wash and set aside. Heat the oil in a wok and when hot, deep fry the catfish till golden and crispy.
2. Wash the vegetables. Peel and wash the shallots then slice finely. Slice the spring onions into small roundels. Finely chop the saw-leaf coriander and Kaffir lime leaves. Pluck the mint leaves and chop roughly.
3. Mix the fish sauce, lime juice, roasted chilli powder and roasted rice powder in a bowl and mix well. Add the fried catfish followed by the Asian shallots and spring onions, the saw-leaf coriander, Kaffir lime leaves and mint.

63

SHRIMP PASTE RICE WITH PRAWN AND PUMPKIN SOUP

Khao kluk kapi kaeng liang kung sod

SHRIMP PASTE RICE
Ingredients
2 cups cooked rice
2 tablespoons red shallots
1 tablespoon chopped garlic
2 tablespoons good quality prawn paste
1 tablespoon sugar
¼ cup dried shrimp crisply fried
2 tablespoons vegetable oil

Heat the oil in a wok and fry the chopped onions and garlic. When they are fragrant add the prawn paste. When all are well mixed, season to taste with sugar. Add the rice and mix thoroughly. Add the crispy fried dried shrimp and mix in. Remove from heat and serve together with all the accompaniments.

Accompaniments
Thinly sliced red shallots
Thinly sliced, peeled unripe mango
Snake beans cut into small roundels
Finely chopped bird's eye chillies
Chinese chicken sausage cut into thin strips
Omelette cut into thin strips
Sweet chicken or pork

SWEET CHICKEN OR PORK
Ingredients
150 grams chicken or pork sliced into
    bite-sized pieces
1 ginger root, peeled and lightly pounded to crush
2 red shallots peeled and lightly pounded
3 cloves crushed garlic
2 coriander roots lightly pounded
5 white peppercorns lightly crushed
5 cups water
2 tablespoons palm sugar
2 tablespoons castor sugar
1 tablespoon white soy sauce
1 teaspoon salt
1 tablespoon dark soy sauce

Fry the pork or chicken in oil in a wok. Add the red shallots, garlic, coriander root and crushed peppercorns. Season to taste with palm sugar, castor sugar, white soy sauce, dark soy sauce and salt. Stir everything to blend well until the meat is cooked. Remove from heat and serve as an accompaniment to the rice.

For Prawn and pumpkin soup see page 153.

64

Khao soi soup
Ingredients
4 chicken drumsticks
¼ cup mashed garlic
¼ cup mashed ginger
¼ cup vegetable oil for frying
1 cup curry paste
2 tablespoons curry powder
1 litre coconut cream
½ litre water
¼ cup white soy sauce
1 tablespoon salt
½ cup sugar

1. Wash the drumsticks and set aside. Heat the oil in a pan and when hot add the garlic and ginger and fry till fragrant. Add the curry paste until it froths up and is fragrant. Then add the curry powder and stir until it is well mixed.
2. Add the chicken thighs, the coconut cream and the water to the pan and bring to a boil. Season to taste with salt, white soy sauce and sugar. Check the taste has well-balanced flavours of salt, sugar and creaminess. Continue simmering until the thighs are cooked (approximately 45 minutes).

Khao soi noodles
Ingredients
1 packet flat egg noodles
1½ litres water
1 litre vegetable oil for frying

1. Bring the water to a boil. Boil half a packet of noodles. Stir to ensure they separate out and do not stick together. When the noodles float to the surface remove with a slotted spoon and rinse before setting aside.
2. Heat the oil in a wok over a high heat. Separate out the other half of the noodles and fry in the hot oil in small batches. Coax the fried noodles into balls. When yellow and crispy, remove from heat and set aside.

NORTHERN STYLE CHICKEN CURRY NOODLES
Khao soi kai

Curry paste
Ingredients
10 dried chillies
10 dried bird's eye chillies
100 grams red shallots
50 grams garlic
1 tablespoon yellow cumin
1 tablespoon of roasted ground ginger
5 peeled and roasted Black Cardamom
1 teaspoon salt
1 teaspoon shrimp paste

67

1. Soak the dried chillies till soft. In a mortar pound the salt, roasted *chago* (black cardamom), roasted cumin and roasted ginger.
2. Add the shallot, garlic, soaked dried chillies and pound finely. Add the shrimp paste and pound till well mixed.

Side dishes
Red shallots chopped into dice, pickled cabbage roughly diced, spring onions finely sliced, halves or quarters of limes, roasted chilli in oil.

How to serve
Place the boiled noodles in a bowl, ladle over the *khao soi* soup and serve one drumstick per bowl. Each person then adds the crispy noodles, pickled cabbage, chopped shallots and chilli in oil to suit their own personal taste.

NOODLE SOUP WITH STEAMED CHICKEN

Kuae tiew kai tun

The Chinese origins of this restorative noodle soup can be seen in the spices required. Although it may seem a bit daunting, all should be fairly readily available.

Ingredients

5 chicken drumsticks, bones removed
5 litres water
1 radish
3 coriander roots
10 white peppercorns
5 star anise flowers
2 sticks cinnamon
½ cup castor sugar
3 tablespoons salt
½ cup white soya sauce
½ cup dark soya sauce
3 spring onions finely sliced
3 coriander plants finely chopped
¼ cup fried garlic
500 grams thin rice noodles
300 grams bean sprouts
300 grams young kale

1. Wash and clean the chicken drumsticks and place in saucepan with 3 litres of water and begin to heat. Crush the garlic and add to the water together with the peppercorns, coriander roots, cinnamon and star anise.

2. Peel the radish and chop into bite-sized pieces. Add to the soup. Bring to a boil and season with salt, sugar, white soya and dark soya. Keep removing any froth that rises to the top. Lower the heat and continue to simmer until the chicken is cooked and tender.

3. Wash the beansprouts and young kale, chopping the latter finely together with the spring onions and coriander.

4. Pour the other 2 litres of water into a saucepan and bring to a boil. Boil the noodles for 1 minute then place them in the individual serving bowls. Add the cabbage and bean sprouts. Pile some chicken on top. Pour over the soup so as to cover the noodles. Sprinkle with the chopped spring onion, coriander and fried garlic. Serve with condiments (sugar, fish sauce, ground roasted chilli, chilli and vinegar, ground peanuts).

68

'RAILWAY' FRIED RICE
Khao phad rod fai

This slightly rough-and-ready version of the ubiquitous fried rice is found the length and breadth of the kingdom, served by food hawkers at train stations, hence the name.

Ingredients
100 grams pork or chicken
50 grams onions
50 grams tomatoes
50 grams kale
200 grams cooked rice
2 eggs
1 teaspoon salt
1 teaspoon ground black pepper
1 tablespoon white soya sauce
1½ tablespoons castor sugar
1 tablespoon dark soya sauce
¼ cup vegetable oil

1. Cut the pork or chicken into thin slices. Peel the onion and chop coarsely. Wash the tomatoes and chop into quarters. Discard the tough outer leaves of kale and chop.
2. Pour the vegetable oil into a wok and place on stove. When it is hot, fry the chicken or pork until cooked. Crack the eggs into the pan and stir until cooked.
3. Add the cooked rice and stir well, then season with salt, sugar, the white and dark soy sauce and the black pepper. Stir well again.
4. Add the onion, kale and tomatoes. When all are cooked, remove from the heat and serve with side dishes of a fried egg for each person, sliced cucumber, spring onions, lime segments, coriander sprigs and bird's eye chilli in fish sauce.

71

APPETIZERS

STUFFED PINEAPPLE SEGMENTS 'GALLOPING HORSES'

Ma ho

Ingredients
pineapple, *ma ho* stuffing, coriander,
    long red finger chilli

Stuffing
1 tablespoon coriander root
1 tablespoon garlic
1 tablespoon black peppercorns
1 cup chopped onion
1 cup chopped pickled white radish
1 cup roasted, chopped peanuts
3 tablespoons palm sugar
3 teaspoons salt
¼ cup vegetable oil for frying

1. Pound together the coriander root, garlic and peppercorns till finely mixed. Heat the oil in a wok and fry for 2 or 3 minutes till fragrant, add the chopped onion, the pickled white radish and the peanuts. Season to taste with palm sugar and salt. Continue frying until well mixed and sticky, capable of being moulded into shape. Set aside.
2. Peel the pineapple, cut into triangular-shaped chunks and scoop out the flesh in the middle. Slice the finger chilli into thin strips; pick off individual coriander leaves. Mould the stuffing into bite-sized balls.
3. Insert the stuffing into the prepared pineapple chunks and decorate with the chilli strips and coriander leaves.

76

TOPPING
Ingredients

3 tablespoons coriander root, garlic
    and peppercorns, finely pounded
500 grams tiger prawns
200 grams minced chicken
1½ cups coconut cream
½ cup roasted chopped peanuts
½ cup castor sugar
1 tablespoon salt
3 tablespoons vegetable oil

1. Finely pound the coriander root, garlic and peppercorns into a paste.
2. Peel the prawns and remove black line. Discard the head and tail and chop the prawns. This should give about 250 grams of prawn meat.
3. Heat the oil in a wok. Fry the coriander root, garlic and peppercorns. When fragrant add the minced chicken and prawns. Cook until done. Don't allow to form into a ball.
4. Add the coconut cream and simmer till it thickens. Season to taste with salt and sugar to achieve the right mix of sweet and salty.
5. Add the chopped peanuts to the wok and mix well.
6. Spoon topping onto the crispy rice crackers. Decorate with coriander and sliced red chilli.

RICE CRACKERS WITH CREAMY PRAWN TOPPING
Khao tang na tang

CRISPY RICE CRACKERS
Cook the rice until slightly soggy. Press the cooked rice into thin shapes either round or square and leave to dry. Then fry in very hot oil until they swell up and are crispy.

79

LEAFY BITES
Miang kum

MIANG KUM SAUCE
Ingredients
1 tablespoon shrimp paste
3 tablespoons palm sugar
1 tablespoon fish sauce
1 tablespoon well-pounded ginger
1 tablespoon well-pounded dried shrimp

Ingredients for the Miang Kum
8 coral tree leaves
8 tablespoons dried shrimp
1 tablespoon diced fresh ginger
1 tablespoon diced red shallot
1 tablespoon diced lime
1 tablespoon roasted unsalted peanuts
1 tablespoon bird's eye chilli finely chopped
1 tablespoon roasted, grated coconut

1. Pound the ginger and dried shimp until well mixed.
2. Take the ginger, dried shrimp, shrimp paste, palm sugar and fish sauce and heat over a low flame until well mixed and slightly thick. Set aside.
3. Take a coral tree leaf and form into a cone. Take a teaspoon and add some sauce.
4. Take an equal pinch of each ingredient and add to the leaf.
5. Fold over the top of the leaf and secure with a toothpick for easy eating.
6. Alternatively place each ingredient in an individual dish and allow the guests to mix their own leafy bites.

Part of the pleasure of this leafy snack is in assembling all the ingredients and making a neat parcel. Thai shops do get deliveries of the leaves on occasion — otherwise lettuce can be substituted.

GOLDEN BUNDLES
Thung thong

Ingredients

4 sheets spring roll pastry
15 prawns
1 teaspoon coriander root
1 teaspoon garlic
1 teaspoon peppercorns
½ tablespoon sugar
1 teaspoon salt
2 spring onions
½ litre vegetable oil
Plum dipping sauce

1. Peel the prawns, remove the black line. Pat dry, chop finely and set aside.
2. Simmer the spring onions until done. These are for tying up the bags.
3. Pound together the coriander root, garlic and peppercorns until well mixed. Mix with the chopped prawns and season with sugar and salt.
4. Cut the sheets of spring roll pastry into squares roughly 4 x 4 inches (this will provide about 16 squares).
5. Spoon a bite-sized amount of the prawn mixture onto each square. Bring the four corners into the centre and make a small bundle; secure with a strand of spring onion.
6. Heat the oil in a pan. When hot fry the bundles until golden and crisp. Serve with plum dipping sauce.

83

EGG LATTICE OMELETTES
La tieng

EGG LATTICE
Components
Egg net (see page 193)
Stuffing
Sprigs of coriander and red finger chilli
    finely sliced

MAKING THE EGG LATTICE
1. Beat the eggs together and sieve through
   a muslin cloth. (This makes creating the
   lattice possible.)
2. Take a frying pan and wipe the surface lightly
   with oil. Set on a low heat. Pour some of the
   egg mixture into a cone, ideally a banana
   leaf, but if not available, use an icing funnel.
   Create a lattice on the pan. Be careful to
   ensure it is just cooked, not crispy, otherwise
   you cannot fold it. Set aside and cover to
   prevent it crisping up.

STUFFING
Ingredients
1 tablespoon coriander root
1 tablespoon garlic
1 tablespoon peppercorns
½ cup red shallot
15 tiger prawns
2 tablespoons castor sugar
2 teaspoons salt

1. Pound the coriander root, garlic and
   peppercorns into a fine paste.
2. Peel the prawns, slice along the back and
   clean before simmering until cooked.
   Pound until fine.
3. Slice the shallot finely.
4. Heat the oil in a wok until hot. Fry the
   coriander root, garlic and peppercorns
   until fragrant, add the chopped onion until
   cooked, add the pounded prawns. Season to
   taste with sugar and salt. Set aside.
5. Take the egg net, lay strips of chilli and
   coriander leaves followed by the filling.
   Fold into bite-sized pieces.

84

CHICKEN SAKU
Ingredients
Tapioca flour, chicken stuffing, accompanying vegetables, fried garlic

TAPIOCA FLOUR
Ingredients
1 cup white tapioca pearls
¼ cup dried butterfly pea flowers
½ cup water
1 tablespoon lime juice

1. Pour the water into a pan and bring to a boil. Add the dried flowers and boil for 5 minutes, sieve through muslin. Add the lime juice and mix well. Set aside the purple flower water.
2. Mix the tapioca pearls with the flower water and set aside covered with a cloth.

CHICKEN STUFFING
Ingredients
1 tablespoon coriander root
1 tablespoon garlic
1 tablespoon black pepper
300 grams chicken breast
2 tablespoons cooking oil
2 teaspoons salt
2 tablespoons sugar

1. Pound the coriander root, garlic and peppercorns into a smooth paste. Heat the water in a pan and cook the chicken breast cut into bite-sized chunks. Set aside to dry.
2. Pound the cooked chicken. Heat the oil in a wok and fry the coriander root, garlic and peppercorn paste until fragrant. Add the diced chicken. Season to taste with salt and sugar. Stir to mix thoroughly.
3. Divide the tapioca mixture into bite-sized balls. Make a hole in the centre and fill with the chicken stuffing, then squeeze the tapioca pastry tightly to close.

CHICKEN AND VEGETARIAN TAPIOCA DUMPLINGS
Saku sai kai, sai mungsavirat

4. Steam the tapioca chicken dumplings until cooked (approx. 5-10 minutes). Serve with accompanying vegetables: cabbage, coriander, bird's eye chillies and fried garlic.

VEGETARIAN STUFFING
The tapioca flour is mixed as before but without the flower water. These dumplings will be white.

Ingredients
1 tablespoon coriander root
½ cup chopped onion
½ cup chopped dried radish
½ cup roasted and pulverised peanuts
1 tablespoon garlic
1 tablespoon black pepper
¼ cup palm sugar
1 tablespoon salt
2 tablespoons cooking oil

1. Pound the coriander root, garlic and peppercorns to a smooth paste. Fry in some oil until fragrant. Add the chopped onion, chopped radish and peanuts. Season to taste with palm sugar and salt. Fry everything together until sticky and mould into balls. Check taste.
2. Divide the tapioca mixture into bite-sized balls. Make a hole in the centre and fill with the vegetarian stuff, then close the hole with the tapioca pastry. Make sure the case is not too thick as it won't be tasty.
3. Place the dumplings in a steamer. Cook until done. Serve with accompaniments as above.

87

'GOLDEN BATS'

Kang kaw thong

Ingredients
Pastry, stuffing, vegetable oil for frying,
plum dipping sauce

PASTRY
Ingredients
½ cup steamed pumpkin
1 cup rice flour
2 tablespoons tapioca flour

Sieve the steamed pumpkin to obtain finely
ground flesh. Mix with the two flours. Knead
well. You will have a golden yellow pastry. Rest.

STUFFING
Ingredients
1 cup diced potatoes
1 cup chopped onion
1 tablespoon coriander root
1 tablespoon garlic
1 tablespoon peppercorns
3 tablespoons curry powder
3 tablespoons sugar
1 tablespoon salt

1. Pound the coriander root, garlic and
   peppercorns to a fine paste. Fry in oil until
   fragrant.
2. Add the onion and diced potatoes and fry
   until cooked. Add the curry powder and mix
   in well. Season to taste with sugar and salt.
3. Divide the pastry into bite-sized portions
   using your fingers to press it into round
   shapes. Spoon in the stuffing and fold in the
   pastry so the stuffing is enclosed.
4. Mould the pastries into triangular shapes.
   Deep fry in plenty of oil until crispy. Serve
   with plum dipping sauce.

88

CHICKEN AND BEEF SATEH

Sateh kai, sateh neua

Ingredients for the skewers

200 grams chicken or beef
½ cup coconut cream
1 tablespoon chopped galangal
2 tablespoons chopped lemongrass
1 tablespoon chopped cumin
½ tablespoon chopped coriander root
½ tablespoon roasted coriander seeds
½ tablespoon roasted cumin seeds
1 teaspoon peppercorns
2 tablespoons castor sugar
2 teaspoons salt

1. Slice the chicken or beef into thin slices approximately 1 x 6 cms.
2. Pound the galangal, lemongrass, cumin, coriander root, roasted coriander seed, roasted cumin seed, peppercorns and salt into a smooth paste.
3. Mix the spices with the coconut cream and season to taste with the sugar and salt. Then add the chicken or beef, mix thoroughly and marinade for a while before threading onto bamboo skewers. Set aside.
4. Grill the skewers until cooked. Serve with peanut sauce and *ajaad*.

Ajaad-cucumber+onion
Ingredients

1 cup castor sugar
1 cup white vinegar
1 tablespoon salt
3 cucumbers [Thai green and white cucumbers are much smaller than European ones so adjust quantities accordingly]
3 red shallots
1 red finger chilli
1 bunch coriander

1. Take the sugar, vinegar and salt and simmer till it thickens slightly. Remove from heat and allow to cool.
2. Quarter the cucumbers and chop into pieces as shown in the photo.
3. Peel the shallots and cut into similar sized pieces to the cucumber.
4. Halve the chilli, remove seeds and chop to same size. Mix all three together and sprinkle with coriander.
5. Pour the sauce over the chopped vegetables before serving.

Peanut-dipping sauce
Ingredients

½ cup finely ground peanuts
2 tablespoons Massaman curry paste
1 tablespoon roasted chilli sauce
1 cup coconut cream
3 tablespoons palm sugar
2 tablespoons tamarind sauce
3 teaspoons salt

Gently simmer all the ingredients until they thicken slightly. Check that the taste has three flavours – sweet, sour and salty.

91

VEGETARIAN RICE FLOUR DUMPLINGS

Khao krieb pak moh

DUMPLING MIXTURE
Ingredients
1 cup rice flour
¼ William's arrow root flour
¼ tapioca flour
½ cup coconut cream
3 cups water

STUFFING
Ingredients
1 tablespoon coriander root
1 tablespoon garlic
1 tablespoon peppercorns
1 cup chopped onion
1 cup chopped dried radish
1 cup roasted and ground peanuts
3 tablespoons palm sugar
3 teaspoons salt
¼ cup vegetable oil

ACCOMPANYING VEGETABLES
Iceberg lettuce, coriander, bird's eye chillies, fried garlic

1. Pound the coriander root, garlic and peppercorns into a fine paste. Heat some oil in the wok and fry till fragrant. Then add the chopped onions, dried radish and the pulverised roasted peanuts. Season to taste with palm sugar and salt. Stir until all the ingredients are well combined and mould into small balls. Set aside.
2. Mix the different flours with the water and the coconut cream. Sieve and set aside.
3. Prepare a pan to make the dumplings. Pour in water to around half full. Stretch some muslin or cotton across the mouth of the pan and make a hole for the steam to escape. Bring to a boil.
4. Spread a roundel of pastry on the stretched cloth. Take care it is not too thick. Cover with the lid of the pan for about 15 seconds when it will be cooked. Open the lid, put one of the moulded stuffings in the middle and fold the pastry to enclose. Remove at once and set aside until all are done.
5. Serve with accompaniment vegetables.

CRISPY WRAPPED PRAWNS AND MACKEREL MIANG

Kung hom sabai miang pla tu

Ingredients for the prawns

3 slices spring roll pastry wrapping
12 tiger prawns
1 teaspoon coriander root
1 teaspoon garlic
1 teaspoon ground pepper
1 teaspoon salt
1 teaspoon sugar
4 tablespoons plum dipping sauce
½ litre vegetable oil for frying

1. Peel the prawns, slice down the back and clean. Straighten the prawns as much as possible.
2. Finely pound the coriander roots, garlic and black pepper and mix with the prawns. Season to taste with salt and sugar. Set aside.
3. Cut the spring roll pastry squares into four.
4. Wrap each prawn in one piece of spring roll pastry.
5. Heat the oil in a pan on the stove and when hot deep fry the prawns until the outside pastry is golden and crisp (approx. 10-15 mins).

Ingredients for mackerel miang

4 sheets fresh spring roll pastry wrap
1 mackerel [a smoked mackerel fillet can substitute]
4 iceberg lettuce leaves
50 grams holy basil
50 grams mint
80 grams Thai rice noodles [khanom chin]
¼ litre vegetable oil for frying

1. Lightly fry the mackerel so that it is cooked but not crisp.
2. Wash the lettuce, basil and mint. Shake off the water and allow to dry.
3. Soak the fresh spring roll wraps in warm water one sheet at a time. When they have softened place on a chopping board or flat surface.
4. Place a lettuce leaf on top of the spring roll pastry followed by a basil leaf, mint and some mackerel flesh and a few pieces of khanom chin. Roll into a cylinder like a spring roll.
5. Cut the rolled cylinder into bite-sized pieces and serve with a seafood dipping sauce.

Ingredients for the seafood sauce

1 tablespoon coriander root
1 tablespoon garlic
1 tablespoon green bird's eye chilli
1½ tablespoons lime juice
1½ tablespoons fish sauce
1½ tablespoons sugar

Place all the ingredients in a blender and blitz finely. Taste to ensure a good mix.

95

GREEN CHILLI SALAD, DRIED SHRIMP AND BOILED EGG

Prik yum kung haeng khai tom

Ingredients
5 red shallots
2 tablespoons dried shrimp
2 bird's eye chillies
4 long green chillies
2 tablespoons fish sauce
2 tablespoons lime juice
I teaspoon sugar
16 quails' eggs

1. Grill the green chillies until they are cooked. Peel the skin and then slice finely discarding the seeds.
2. Boil the quails' eggs for around IO minutes. Remove and plunge in cold water, then peel and set aside.
3. Pound the dried shrimp finely and set aside. Finely chop the bird's eye chillies. Peel and halve the shallots, then slice into thin roundels.
4. Place the sliced shallots in a bowl together with the fish sauce, the lime juice, the sugar and the finely chopped bird's eye chilli. Mix until the sugar is dissolved then add the finely sliced long green chillies. Toss so all the flavours are combined and serve atop halved quails' eggs.

MINIATURE 'SON-IN-LAW' EGGS
Khai look koei krae

This recipe is more commonly found made with hens' eggs, but the version using quail's eggs is more elegant and can be used as a cocktail snack.

Ingredients
12 quails' eggs
50 grams finely chopped red shallots
¼ cup tamarind water
¼ cup palm sugar
3 tablespoons fish sauce
¼ litre vegetable oil for frying

1. Hard boil the quails' eggs (about 10 minutes), plunge in cold water and then peel. Fry in the vegetable oil until they are golden. Set aside.
2. Divide the chopped shallots in two. Fry half in the oil until they are golden and crispy.
3. Fry the other half in shallow oil until they are fragrant. Add the tamarind water, palm sugar, fish sauce and heat until they are well combined. Make sure all three flavours are discernable – sour, sweet and salty.
4. Place the fried quails' eggs in a serving dish, dribble over the tamarind sauce and sprinkle with the fried onions.

99

COCKTAILS

TOM YUM PUNCH
Punch tom yum

Ingredients
2 Kaffir limes
5 stalks lemongrass
1 root galangal
5 Kaffir lime leaves
2 red finger chillies
½ cup lime juice
½ cup castor sugar
2 tablespoons salt
1 litre soda water
1 litre water
2 kilograms of ice cubes

102

1. Wash the ingredients.
2. Halve the Kaffir limes. Pound the bulb of the lemongrass stalk and cut into approximately 1½ inch lengths. Peel and slice the galangal into 3 mm roundels, halve the finger chilli and de-seed. Tear the Kaffir lime leaves into large pieces.
3. Place all the ingredients in a punch bowl. Add the lime juice, sugar, salt, soda and plain water. Stir gently to dissolve the sugar and salt. Add the ice cubes and serve.

These Thai drinks are simple to make and when served with ice are very refreshing. In addition their vivid but natural colours are very inviting. They do use a lot of sugar but in a hot climate, a cool sugary drink is often a necessary pick-me-up.

ROSELLA WITH SODA
Ingredients
200 grams dried rosella flowers
2 litres water
500 grams castor sugar
½ litre soda

1. Wash the dried flowers to remove any dust and place in a pan with the water. Bring to a boil, before adding the sugar. Boil for another 25 minutes, then remove from the heat and allow to cool.
2. Strain the flowers and liquid through a white muslin cloth and store in the fridge.
3. When serving use equal quantities of rosella water and soda.

VARIATION: To make an alcoholic drink, use one measure of vodka or gin, one measure of lime juice in a tall glass, top with equal amounts of soda and rosella plus a few mint leaves – delicious!

LEMONGRASS SQUASH
Ingredients
1 kilogram lemongrass
200 grams fresh pandanus leaves
500 grams castor sugar
5 litres water

1. Wash the lemongrass and pandanus leaves, before chopping finely.
2. Pour the water into a pan and bring to a boil. First add the pandanus leaves and boil for around 5 minutes before adding the lemongrass and boil until fragrant – about 30 minutes.

3. Add the sugar and stir to dissolve. Boil for a further 5 minutes.
4. Remove the lemongrass and pandanus leaves and strain the liquid through a muslin cloth. Allow to cool and store in the fridge.

PANDANUS SQUASH
Ingredients
2 kilograms pandanus leaves
500 grams castor sugar
5 litres water

1. Wash and chop 1 kg pandanus leaves.
2. Chop the remaining leaves and blend in a food mixer with ½ litre water.
3. Pour the remaining water into a pan, set on the stove and bring to a boil. Add the chopped leaves and boil for 10 minutes, or until fragrant.
4. Add the sugar and stir to dissolve before adding the blended pandanus leaves. Continue boiling for another 5 minutes and a beautiful green liquid will result.
5. Remove from the heat, spoon out the leaves and strain the liquid through muslin. Allow to cool and store in the fridge.

BALE FRUIT SQUASH
Ingredients
500 grams dried, sliced bale fruit
500 grams castor sugar
5 litres water

1. Wash the bale fruit and place in a pan with the water. Bring to the boil and add the castor sugar.
2. Boil for around 25 minutes until the liquid is slightly sticky. Strain through muslin, allow to cool and store in the fridge.

105

DINNER

CRISPY HERB SPICY SALAD
Yum samun prai krob

Ingredients
50 grams roselle shoots
50 grams olive shoots
5 wild pepper leaves
30 grams Thai basil
30 grams sweet basil
1 head ginger
50 grams carrot
30 grams centella
2 stems lemongrass
3 red bird's eye chillies
4 red shallots
3 spring onions
3 tablespoons fish sauce
3 tablespoons sugar
3 tablespoons lime juice
½ cup batter [see page 192,
    or use tempura batter]
2 litres oil for frying

1. Carefully wash all the herbs and vegetables, and toss dry. Cut the wild pepper, the roselle shoots, olive shoots, leaves, Thai basil leaves, sweet basil leaves and vegetables into thin strips. Place in a mixing bowl. Peel the ginger, cut into thin roundels and then slice finely. Peel the carrots and slice finely. Slice the lemongrass into small roundels. Add to the sliced herbs and gently toss all together so they are well mixed.

2. Mix in the batter to cover all the ingredients. Pour the oil into a wok and set on a high heat. Deep fry the herbs until crispy and use a slotted spoon to remove. Dry off oil.

3. For the yum sauce, pour the fish sauce and sugar into a pan and heat until the sugar dissolves. Remove from the heat and add the lime juice, mixing well.

4. Peel the onions, wash and halve before slicing finely. Wash the spring onions and slice crossways into small roundels. Chop the bird's eye chillies.

5. Mix the yum sauce and chopped onion, spring onions and chillies together. Serve alongside the crispy herbs. Do not pour over before serving as they will become soggy.

POMELO SALAD
WITH CRAB MEAT

Yum som-o neua pu

Ingredients

20 coral tree leaves
200 grams peeled and segmented pomelo
50 grams crab meat
3 Kaffir lime leaves
¼ cup fried red shallot
¼ cup roasted grated coconut
¼ cup roasted crushed peanuts
10 young wild pepper leaves

1. Peel and break the pomelo into small segments. Finely slice the Kaffir lime leaves. Mix the two together and set aside.
2. Steam the crab meat for about 5 minutes until cooked. Set aside to cool. Wash the coral tree leaves and arrange them on the serving dish.
3. Gently mix in the *yum* dressing and the pomelo. Add the fried shallots, roasted coconut and roasted crushed peanuts and mix carefully together. Spoon the pomelo mixture onto the betel leaves. Top with the steamed crab meat and decorate with coriander leaves and finely sliced long red chillies before serving.

YUM DRESSING
Ingredients

4-5 dried fried bird's eye chillies
20 grams coriander leaves
20 grams finely sliced long red finger chillies
½ cup finely crushed peanuts
1 tablespoon toasted galangal
1 tablespoon toasted lemongrass
2 tablespoons roasted shredded coconut
2 tablespoons roasted chilli sauce
3 tablespoons palm sugar
3 tablespoons fish sauce
3 tablespoons lime juice

113

Take the sliced and toasted galangal, the finely sliced and toasted lemongrass, the shredded coconut and pound together until well mixed. Combine with the roasted chilli sauce, palm sugar, fish sauce and lime juice. Heat gently over a low flame until it begins to thicken and allow to cool.

FRIED PLA SALID *(Trichogaster pectoralis)*
WITH GREEN MANGO SALAD
Pla salid tod yum mamuang

This large freshwater species is farmed in the marshes near Samutprakhan. When I was a child, I loved seeing the fish hanging up to dry. Deep fried and crispy, they are like the so-called 'Bombay duck' of India, the salty crispness contrasts perfectly with the sour, clean taste of unripe mango.

114

Ingredients
100 grams deep fried *pla salid*
1 unripe mango
4 red shallots
3 spring onions
3 red bird's eye chillies
¼ cup fried red shallots
¼ cup fried cashew nuts
1 bunch coriander
1 long red chilli
¼ cup fish sauce
¼ cup sugar
1 tablespoon lime juice

1. Fillet the *pla salid* flesh from the bones. Deep fry in vegetable oil. Then fry the cashew nuts. Peel the mango and slice finely (you can use a julienne peeler). Peel then finely slice the shallots, spring onions and bird's eye chillies. Pick the coriander leaves into small sprigs. Slice the long chilli into thin strips.

2. Take a pan and heat the fish sauce and sugar until the latter dissolves. Remove from the heat and when almost cool, add the lime juice, stirring well to mix.

3. Add the chopped bird's eye chilli to the *yum* sauce and then add the chopped red shallots and green mango. Finally, add the crispy fish and fried cashew nuts. Toss everything gently to mix and serve garnished with sprigs of coriander and finely sliced long red chilli.

SPICY SEAFOOD SALAD

Pla talae ruam

Ingredients

100 grams prawns
100 grams cuttlefish
100 grams mussels
100 grams crab thighs
50 grams red shallots
50 grams lemongrass
50 grams mint
2 bird's eye chillies
2 Kaffir lime leaves
1 tablespoon roasted chilli oil
2 tablespoons lime juice
2 tablespoons fish sauce
2 teaspoons palm sugar

1. Peel the prawns, make an incision along the back and clean thoroughly. Simmer till tender. Clean and slice the cuttlefish into bite-sized portions, simmer till tender. Simmer the mussels and when cooked remove from the shell. Cook the crab thighs and set aside.
2. Slice the shallots finely and the lemongrass into roundels. Pluck the mint into individual leaves. Finely slice the bird's eye chillies and the Kaffir lime leaves.
3. Mix together the roasted chilli oil, the lime juice, sugar and chopped chillies. Add the seafood ingredients, followed by the sliced shallots, lemongrass, mint and Kaffir lime leaves. Toss all the ingredients together. Check seasoning and serve.

117

GRILLED LONG AUBERGINE SALAD

Yum makeua yaw

Ingredients

3 long green aubergines
4 tiger prawns
4 red shallots
2 spring onions
30 grams mint
3 red bird's eye chillies
I tablespoon dried shrimp
3 tablespoons fish sauce
3 tablespoons sugar
3 tablespoons lime juice
I red finger chilli

118

1. If possible grill the aubergines over charcoal, otherwise use the grill. Make sure they are cooked through. When cool, peel and set aside in the fridge.
2. Place the egg in boiling water and hard boil (Note: don't overcook as the colour of the yolk will be less attractive). Peel and set aside.
3. Finely pound the dried shrimp and set aside to use as a topping.
4. Cook the fresh tiger prawns for I minute in boiling water.
5. Peel the shallots, wash, halve, then slice finely. Chop the red bird's eye chillies. Wash and finely chop the spring onions into small roundels. Pick the mint leaves off the stem keeping the top leaves for decoration. Halve the finger chilli lengthwise, remove any flesh and seeds, then slice into thin strips.
6. Pour the fish sauce and the sugar into a saucepan and bring to a boil. Stir until the sugar dissolves. Remove from the heat and add lime juice.
7. Cut the aubergine into pieces around 2 inches long and arrange on a dish. Thoroughly mix together the *yum* sauce, the chopped bird's eye chilli, the chopped spring onion and the mint leaves. Pour the sauce over the aubergines. Before serving decorate with sliced boiled egg, cooked tiger prawns, pounded dried shrimp, the tips of the mint stalks and the thinly sliced finger chilli.

LEMONGRASS AND TIGER PRAWN YUM

Yum takrai kung sod

Ingredients
10 tiger prawns
4 stems lemongrass
4 red shallots
1 bulb ginger
3 spring onions
1 bunch sawtooth coriander
30 grams mint
3 Kaffir lime leaves
4 red bird's eye chillies
8 wild pepper leaves
¼ cup fish sauce
¼ cup sugar
¼ cup lime juice
1 bunch coriander
1 red finger chilli

1. Peel the prawns, remove the black line and wash. Set aside in the fridge. Peel the shallots, wash and split in half before finely chopping lengthwise. Remove outer leaves of lemongrass keeping only the young, white parts and slice into thin roundels; peel the ginger, cut into thin slices and then into long strips; wash the spring onions and sawtooth coriander and chop together. Cut the Kaffir lime leaves into long strips. Pluck the mint into individual leaves. Finely chop the red bird's eye chillies. Wash the wild pepper leaves ready to be laid on the plate as a base. Pick the coriander into small bunches. Slice the red finger chillies into thin strips to decorate the top.

2. Pour the fish sauce and sugar into a saucepan and heat till the sugar dissolves. Remove from the heat and mix in the lime juice.

3. Boil water in a pan, add the prawns and gently simmer until they are just cooked (approx. 1 minute). Remove and plunge into iced water and drain.

4. Place the prawns in a dish, add the sliced onions, ginger, lemongrass and bird's eye chilli. Pour on the *yum* sauce and mix thoroughly. Then add the spring onion, sawtooth coriander, Kaffir lime leaves and mint. Mix well. Season to taste.

5. Spread the pepper leaves on a serving platter, spoon the *yum* on top and decorate with coriander and thinly sliced finger chillies.

121

WINGED BEAN SALAD WITH BOILED EGG

Yum tua pu khai tom

Ingredients
150 grams winged beans
50 grams red shallots
2 red bird's eye chillies
¼ cup dry fried grated coconut
¼ cup ground peanuts
¼ cup fried shallots
1 cup *yum* sauce for salad
2 hard-boiled eggs
2 red finger chillies
4 fried dried chillies
1 bunch coriander

YUM SAUCE
Ingredients
2 tablespoons roasted chilli sauce
¼ cup coconut cream
¼ cup palm sugar
¼ cup fish sauce
¼ cup lime juice

1. Heat the ingredients for the *yum* dressing and stir thoroughly. Once it has come to a boil remove from heat and set aside.
2. Lightly boil the winged beans. Refresh in cold water and slice thinly. Finely slice the red shallots, bird's eye and finger chillies. Tear off some coriander leaves to garnish.
3. Put all the ingredients in a bowl. Drizzle with the *yum* sauce. Mix together thoroughly and transfer to a serving dish. Decorate with sliced hard-boiled eggs, fried dried chillies, coriander and finely sliced red finger chillies.

RIVER PRAWN DRY CURRY

Chu chi kung maenam

Ingredients

5 river prawns
½ cup mixed rice and wheat flour
5 bamboo skewers
I litre vegetable oil
½ cup curry paste
I cup coconut cream
I tablespoon rice flour
I tablespoon fish sauce
I½ tablespoons sugar
2 Kaffir lime leaves
I bunch coriander
I red finger chilli

1. Tear some Kaffir lime leaves and cut into fine strips (see page 190). Halve the finger chilli and remove seeds. Divide the coriander into small sprigs for decoration on top.
2. Prepare the river prawns by removing the back legs. Peel and remove the black line along the back. Skewer with a bamboo stick to prevent the prawn from curling during frying.
3. Pour the oil into a pan and heat. Lightly coat with flour. When cooked (3-4 mins), remove and set aside.
4. Heat the oil and fry the curry paste until fragrant. Add the coconut cream (while keeping around 4 tablespoons back). Stir thoroughly and season to taste with fish sauce before taking off the heat.
5. Take the remaining coconut cream and mix with the rice flour. Place in a pan over the heat and stir until the flour is cooked and the coconut cream has thickened. Remove from the heat.

6. Remove the bamboo skewers and arrange the prawns on a serving dish. Spoon the *chu-chi* sauce over the prawns and add the coconut cream. Decorate with the finely sliced Kaffir lime leaves, coriander sprigs and finely sliced finger chilli.

CHU CHI CURRY PASTE

Ingredients

10 dried finger chillies
I tablespoon coriander root
¼ cup chopped red shallots
¼ cup chopped garlic
I tablespoon galangal sliced into roundels
3 tablespoons chopped lemongrass
I teaspoon Kaffir lime zest
I teaspoon peppercorns
I teaspoon salt
I teaspoon shrimp paste

1. Soak the dried chillies until soft.
2. Pound the salt, galangal and peppercorns into a fine paste. Add the coriander root and the lime zest.
3. Add the soaked chillies, followed by the garlic, onion and lemongrass. Pound everything until smooth. Finally add the shrimp paste and pound until everything is well combined.

See also pages 188-189.

125

BEEF GREEN CURRY WITH BIRD'S EYE CHILLIES

Kaeng khiew wan neua prik khi nu

Ingredients

300 grams beef (sirloin)

100 grams round aubergines

50 grams pea aubergines

3 Kaffir lime leaves

2 red finger chillies

1 tablespoon bird's eye chillies

50 grams holy basil

½ cup green curry paste (see pages 188-189)

3 cups coconut cream

3 tablespoons palm sugar

2 tablespoons fish sauce

1. Slice the beef into bite-sized pieces. Add about one cup of coconut cream to the beef, mix well and marinade for at least 30 minutes.
2. Prepare the other ingredients. Remove the stalks from the round aubergines and slice into quarters. Pick off the pea aubergines and pluck the holy basil leaves. Tear the Kaffir lime leaves into small pieces. Slice the red finger chillies into strips and remove the stalks from the bird's eye chillies.
3. Set the wok on the stove and add one cup of coconut cream. Heat until it separates. Fry the green curry paste until fragrant. Add the beef and stir to mix well. Add the remaining coconut cream and bring to a boil. Add the round aubergines, pea aubergines, sliced finger chillies, Kaffir lime leaves and the bird's eye chillies. Season to taste with palm sugar and fish sauce, then add the holy basil leaves. Stir until the curry is cooked, turn off the heat and spoon into a serving dish. The curry liquid should be slightly thick.

126

CHICKEN CURRY WITH *AJAAD* (cucumber and shallot salad)
Kaeng karee kai ajaad

Ingredients
500 grams chicken drumsticks
(skin and bone removed)
1 large onion
2 waxy potatoes
¼ cup curry paste
1 tablespoon curry powder
3 cups coconut cream
3 tablespoons sugar
1 tablespoon fish sauce

1. Divide the chicken drumsticks (skin and bone removed) into manageable pieces. Marinade in ½ cup of coconut cream. Peel and wash the onions and potatoes before cutting both into approximately 1 inch cubes.
2. Heat one cup of coconut cream in a wok until it separates. Add the curry paste and fry until fragrant. Add the curry powder and stir until it is well mixed.
3. Add remaining coconut cream followed by the marinaded chicken, the onions and potatoes. Season to taste with fish sauce and sugar. Bring to a boil and simmer until the potatoes are cooked. Check seasoning again, then spoon into serving dish and serve with *ajaad*.

Ingredients for the *ajaad*
1 cup castor sugar
1 cup white vinegar
1 tablespoon salt
3 cucumbers (small Thai ones, or 1 larger European one)
3 red shallots
1 red finger chilli
1 bunch coriander leaves

Place the sugar, vinegar and salt in a small pan and heat until the mixture thickens slightly. Set aside to cool. Slice the cucumbers into quarters lengthwise and chop reasonably finely. Peel and chop the shallots, deseed the chilli and chop both into similar-sized pieces. Garnish with coriander leaves and pour the *ajaad* sauce over the chopped vegetebles before serving.

129

Ingredients for the curry paste
15 dried red finger chillies
¼ cup red shallots
¼ cup garlic
1 tablespoon ginger
1 tablespoon coriander seeds
1 tablespoon cumin seeds
1 tablespoon curry powder
1 teaspoon sliced tumeric
1 teaspoon salt

1. Soak the dried chillies in water until soft. Toast the coriander and cumin seeds until fragrant and set aside. Peel the garlic and shallots and chop roughly. Peel the ginger and tumeric and slice into roundels.
2. Place the salt, the toasted coriander seeds and cumin in a mortar and pound finely. Add the tumeric and ginger and pound further. Add the shallots and garlic and pound until fine. Then add the soaked dried chillies and again pound finely. Lastly add the curry powder and pound all the ingredients into a fine paste. Remove from the mortar and reserve in a dish in the fridge.

BEEF MASSAMAN CURRY WITH LOTUS SEEDS

Massaman neua med bua

Ingredients

400 grams beef (shin)
200 grams potatoes (waxy ones are best)
50 grams large onions
30 grams lotus seeds
20 grams red shallots, fried
1 tablespoon turmeric powder
½ cup Massaman curry paste
4 tablespoons palm sugar
4 tablespoons fish sauce
2 tablespoons tamarind sauce
4 cups coconut cream

1. Chop beef into 2 inch cubes. Braise the meat in water until tender (approx. 1½-2 hrs). Set aside.
2. Peel and cut the potatoes into cubes similar in size to the meat. Peel and quarter the onions.
3. Heat one cup coconut cream till it separates. Fry the curry paste until fragrant and then add the turmeric. Stir over a medium to low heat taking care the paste does not burn.
4. Add the onions, potatoes and lotus seeds and fry (approx. 2 mins). Add the remaining coconut cream. Stir until the liquid bubbles. Season with fish sauce, sugar and tamarind sauce. Then add the boiled beef to the curry and simmer until the potatoes are cooked. Sprinkle with fried shallots and serve.

130

ROAST DUCK CURRY WITH FRESH GRAPES
Kaeng ped phed yang a-ngun sod

Ingredients
½ roast duck
5 round aubergines
I cup pea aubergines
10 cherry tomatoes
¼ cup sliced pineapple
15 black grapes
2 red finger chillies
4 Kaffir lime leaves
100 grams sweet basil leaves
2 cups coconut cream
I cup curry paste
I cup palm sugar
3 tablespoons fish sauce

1. Debone the duck and chop into bite-sized pieces. Wash the vegetables and prepare, cutting off the stem of the aubergine and slicing. Remove the pineapple skin and cut into bite-sized pieces. Slice the red finger chillies diagonally. Tear the Kaffir lime leaves into small pieces and pluck the basil into individual leaves.
2. Place half a cup of cocunut cream into a wok and heat until it separates. Add the curry paste and stir gradually, cooking until fragrant. Add the pineapple and mix well with the curry sauce.
3. Add the remaining coconut cream and bring to a boil. Add the duck, the aubergine, pea aubergines, grapes, red chillies and Kaffir lime leaves. Season to taste with palm sugar and fish sauce. Finally add the basil leaves, stir thoroughly, take off the heat and serve. You can substitute lychees for grapes if desired.

CURRY PASTE
Ingredients
10 dried finger chillies
20 red bird's eye chillies
I tablespoon coriander root
¼ cup sliced red shallots
¼ cup garlic
I tablespoon galangal sliced in roundels
3 tablespoons lemongrass finely sliced
I teaspoon Kaffir lime zest
I teaspoon peppercorns
I teaspoon roasted coriander seeds
I teaspoon roasted turmeric
I teaspoon salt
I teaspoon shrimp paste

1. Soften the dried chillies in water. Pound the salt, galangal and peppercorns finely, add the roasted coriander, roasted turmeric, coriander root and Kaffir lime zest and pound to a fine paste.
2. Pound the bird's eye chillies one at a time till fine before pounding the soaked dried chillies, followed by the garlic, red onions and lemongrass. Make sure all the ingredients are blended into a smooth paste. Finally add the shrimp paste until everything is well mixed.

133

FRIED FISH-PASTE BALLS
Tod mun pla krai

Ingredients for the fish-paste balls
300 grams filleted fish
100 grams red curry paste
150 grams winged beans, finely sliced
5 Kaffir lime leaves finely sliced
I egg
I tablespoon coriander root
I tablespoon garlic
I tablespoon peppercorns
I tablespoon castor sugar
I teaspoon salt

1. Pound the coriander root, garlic and peppercorns into a smooth paste.
2. In a bowl mix together the red curry paste (see page 189), egg, coriander root, garlic, black peppercorns, castor sugar and salt.
3. Add the fish to the mixture and use a spoon to knead all the ingredients together until sticky.
4. Add the chopped winged beans and finely sliced Kaffir lime leaves and mix thoroughly. Mould into round balls with a slight indentation on one side.
5. Set a pan of oil over a medium flame. Fry the fish-paste balls until they are cooked (4-5 minutes). Turn them to ensure they are evenly cooked. Remove and set aside, draining any excess oil. Serve with the dipping sauce.

Ingredients for the dipping sauce
I cup castor sugar
I cup white vinegar
I tablespoon salt
2 small cucumbers,
    or ½ large European variety
2 red shallots
I red finger chilli
I spring onion
I bunch coriander
2 tablespoons roasted crushed peanuts

Take the vinegar, sugar and salt and place in a pan. Heat until the liquid begins to reduce. Chop the cucumber, shallots, chilli, spring onion, coriander and combine together in a bowl. Pour over the liquid. Finish by adding the chopped peanuts and mix together well.

STIR-FRIED CRISPY CATFISH

Phad ped pla duk krob

Ingredients

3 small catfish (difficult to substitute but trout is possible)
5 young round aubergines
I level cupful pea eggplant
5 finger root galangal bulbs
2 red finger chillies
½ cupful green peppercorns
5 Kaffir lime leaves
100 grams sweet basil
I cup curry paste (see page 189)
½ cup brown sugar

1. Clean the catfish and remove the mucus by washing several times in salt water (it is clean when no longer slippery). Then cut across the fish crosswise into roundels ½ cm wide without removing the bones. Discard the head. Wash again and set aside. Heat vegetable oil in a wok; when very hot fry the catfish till crispy, remove and dry on kitchen paper.

2. Wash all the vegetables. Quarter the round aubergines. Halve the red finger chillies, remove the seeds and slice diagonally.

3. Finely slice the galangal. Cut the young green peppercorns into small bunches. Tear the Kaffir lime leaves. Pluck the Thai basil into individual leaves.

4. Fry the basil leaves till crispy and set aside. Then fry all the other vegetable ingredients till cooked but not crisp (about 1-2 mins).

5. Place the wok on the stove with ⅓ cup oil, fry the curry paste on a low heat stirring until the paste is well mixed and fragrant (about 1 min). Add fish sauce and sugar to taste. Add the prepared catfish and mix with the curry paste.

6. Add all the vegetable ingredients and toss till well mixed. Add half the crispy basil leaves and mix. Remove from heat and top with remaining basil leaves before serving.

137

YELLOW BEAN DIPPING SAUCE

Lon tao jiew

Ingredients

100 grams fermented soya beans
100 grams red shallots
50 grams lemongrass
30 grams young galangal
2 red finger chillies
2 yellow finger chillies
2 green finger chillies
2 coriander roots
100 grams tiger prawns
2 cups coconut cream
4 tablespoons castor sugar
1 teaspoon salt
1 bunch coriander, plucked in sprigs
1 red finger chilli finely sliced

138

DIPPING VEGETABLES AND FISH

Cabbage, cauliflower, snake beans, cucumber, small purple aubergines, fresh white cumin, crispy fish.

1. Finely slice the shallots, pound the lemongrass and cut into sticks, slice the galangal into thin roundels, wash the coriander roots, slice the finger chillies into sticks, rinse the fermented soya beans in water, clean the prawns removing the black line and chop.
2. Place the coconut cream in a pan and add the lemongrass, galangal, soya and coriander roots. Bring to a boil and add the prawns and the chopped chillies. Be careful the coconut cream does not separate.
3. Season to taste with sugar and salt, then spoon into a bowl. Sprinkle with the coriander sprigs and finely sliced red chilli. Serve with the prepared vegetables which can be carved if desired.
4. Use sea bass for the fried fish which should be filleted and cut into bite-sized pieces. Lightly toss in flour and cook so it is crispy on the outside and soft inside.

CRAB DIPPING SAUCE

Lon pu khai

Ingredients

2 crabs with eggs
5 red shallots
1 stem galangal
3 sticks lemongrass
2 each finger chillies – yellow, green, red
3 coriander roots
1 ½ cups coconut cream
¼ cup sugar
2 tablespoons salt

1. Wash and clean the crab, chopping it into bite-sized pieces. Peel and slice the shallots and galangal finely. Peel off the outside sheath of the lemongrass. Pound to crush lightly then chop into short lengths. Wash the chillies and chop into lengths of about 1 cm. Wash the coriander roots and pound slightly to crush.

2. Place the coconut cream in a pan on the stove. Add the coriander root, chopped shallots, galangal, lemongrass and finger chillies. Then when it has come to a boil, add the crab and season with salt and sugar. Lower the heat and gently simmer until the crab is cooked [about 5 mins]. Spoon the mixture into serving dishes and accompany with vegetables.

ACCOMPANYING VEGETABLES

White cumin
Snake beans
White cabbage
Cucumber
Variously coloured young aubergines

Wash and chop the vegetables and carve attractively.

141

PRAWN DIPPING SAUCE, VEGETABLES AND FRIED MACKEREL

Nam prik kung sod pak sod pla tu tod

Ingredients
10 tiger prawns
8 bird's eye chillies
2 bulbs garlic
1 red shallot
¼ cup pea aubergines
2 tablespoons palm sugar
2 tablespoons lime juice
1 tablespoon shrimp paste
1 teaspoon fish sauce

1. Peel the tiger prawns and remove the black line. Simmer gently in boiling water for about 2 minutes. Remove and set aside.
2. Peel the garlic and shallot, wash the pea aubergines and the bird's eye chillies.
3. Pound the chilli, garlic and shallot till smooth. Add the cooked prawns and the shrimp paste and then the aubergines which should be lightly crushed. Season to taste with palm sugar, lime juice and fish sauce. Serve in small cabbage leaves as shown together with fresh vegetables and fried mackerel.

FRESH VEGETABLES
Cucumber, white cabbage, long green beans, various aubergines, white cumin. Wash all the vegetables and arrange in bite-sized portions. Carve the white cumin if desired.

FRIED MACKEREL
Ingredients
2 small mackerels
½ litre cooking oil

When the oil is sizzling, fry the fish until cooked and crispy. Remove and set aside, then debone and serve with the dipping sauce.

SPICY GRILLED FISH DIPPING SAUCE

Nam prik pla yang

Ingredients for the *nam prik*

1 grilled fish (sea bass or mackerel)
80 grams green and red bird's eye chillies
50 grams red shallots
50 grams garlic
2 tablespoons fish sauce
1 tablespoon lime juice
¼ cup boiled water
1 spring onion
1 bunch coriander

1. Remove the flesh from one grilled fish.
2. Grill the red and green bird's eye chillies, red shallots and garlic until they are fragrant. Then pound finely. Add the fish flesh and mix well.
3. Season with fish sauce, lime juice and add boiled water as neccessary. Mix well, spoon into receptacles and sprinkle with finely chopped coriander and spring onion. Serve with boiled vegetables and boiled egg (make sure the yolk is slightly soft).

BOILED VEGETABLES
Ingredients

1 red sweet potato
1 slice pumpkin (about 100 grams)
4 wild bitter gourd
1 gourds
5 long green beans

1. Peel the red potato and pumpkin and cut into bite-sized pieces, carving them decoratively if desired.
2. Place them in a saucepan and bring to a boil. When cooked remove and plunge into iced water.
3. Boil the small gourds whole and when cooked plunge into iced water. Slice in half and use a spoon to de-seed.
4. Boil the gourd and also plunge into iced water. Cut into bite-sized pieces.
5. Boil the long green beans and when cooked tie into knots and trim ends to make bite-sized pieces.

Boil two duck eggs, stirring them until the water begins to boil. Boil for 10 minutes. Peel and slice into segments before serving.

145

NORTHERN-STYLE DIPPING SAUCE, BLANCHED VEGETABLES, PORK CRACKLING

Nam prik num pak tom kaeb mu

146

Ingredients
100 grams red shallots
100 grams garlic
200 grams green finger chilli
30 grams spring onions
30 grams coriander
¼ cup lime juice
¼ cup fish sauce

VEGETABLES AND PORK CRACKLING FOR DIPPING
Cauliflower, long green beans, small gourd, pumpkin, snake gourd, pink potatoes, pork crackling.

1. Grill the green finger chillies, red shallots, and garlic until cooked and fragrant.
2. Peel the chillies and pound along with the red shallots and garlic until they are quite fine.
3. Add fish sauce to taste and stir in the lime juice. Spoon into small bowls and sprinkle with chopped coriander and spring onions. Serve with the blanched vegetables and pork crackling.
4. The vegetables should be blanched individually and when removed from boiling water plunged into ice cold water. Trim them attractively before serving.

For the crackling, boil the pork skin in slightly salted water until soft. Remove and cut into bite-sized pieces. Lay out to dry. When completely dry, fry in very hot oil until golden and bubbly.

TOM YUM KUNG WITH YOUNG COCONUT

Tom yum kung maenam mapraw on

Ingredients

4 river prawns
100 grams straw mushrooms
30 grams galangal
30 grams lemongrass
2 Kaffir lime leaves
3 bird's eye chillies
20 grams coriander and sawtooth coriander
20 grams spring onions
50 grams red shallots
1 teaspoon castor sugar
1 tablespoon roasted chilli paste
3 tablespoons lime juice
2 cups soup stock
1 young coconut

1. Peel the prawns but keep the shells for stock. Remove the black strip and wash. Slice the straw mushrooms in half, slice the galangal into thin roundels, finely slice the lemongrass. Lightly pound the red shallots to split them and coarsely chop. Lightly crush the chillies. Tear the Kaffir lime leaves into small shreds, removing the stem.
2. To make the stock, boil the prawn shells with the trimmings of the galangal and lemongrass. Simmer for 20 minutes removing any scum that forms. Then strain keeping only the liquid.
3. Set the soup to boil. Add the galangal, lemongrass, Kaffir lime leaves, red shallots and chillies. Simmer until fragrant. Add the roasted chili paste, season to taste with fish sauce, sugar and lime juice.
4. Add the straw mushrooms and prawns. Simmer until just cooked and ladle into bowls. Add the young coconut flesh which has been scooped out in advance. Sprinkle with coriander, parsley and spring onions before serving.

149

GOURD SOUP WITH MINCED PRAWN

Kaeng jeud tamlung kung sup

Ingredients
15 tiger prawns
200 grams ivy gourd shoots
3 cups chicken stock
1 tablespoon fried garlic
1 tablespoon white soya sauce
1 teaspoon salt
½ teaspoon castor sugar
½ teaspoon ground black pepper

1. Pluck the leaves from the ivy gourd shoots. Wash thoroughly.
2. Peel and clean the prawns, then chop finely which should give about 100 grams of minced prawn.
3. Place the chicken stock in a pan over a moderate heat. Bring to the boil and season with salt, white soya sauce and sugar. Add the ivy gourd leaves.
4. Add the chopped prawn, stir to break up and cook for around 1 minute.
5. Spoon the ivy gourd leaves into the bowl first, followed by the minced prawn and ladle over the stock. Sprinkle with crispy fried garlic and black pepper before serving.

CHICKEN STOCK
Ingredients
200 grams chicken bones
1 ½ litres water

Bring the chicken bones in the water to the boil on a high heat for around 5 minutes. Remove any scum that collects. Reduce to medium heat and continue to simmer for 30 minutes. Remove from the heat and strain, reserving the liquid.

CRISPY FRIED GARLIC
Ingredients
100 grams garlic
300 millilitres vegetable oil

Finely chop the garlic. Heat the oil over a medium heat. When the oil is hot (approx. 2 minutes), add the garlic and stir to make sure it cooks evenly (about 5 minutes). When the garlic is cooked, it will float on the surface and turn golden. Remove and dry on kitchen towel.

150

SPICY VEGETABLE SOUP WITH FRESH PRAWNS

Kaeng liang kung sod

In the old days, this spicy vegetable soup was given to women who had just given birth, as it was believed to encourage the flow of milk. Less well known than Tom Yum *or* Tom Kha *soups, it is nevertheless delicious and does feel very healthy.*

Ingredients

8 prawns
1 gourd
10 straw mushrooms
4 sweet corn tips or baby corns
100 grams pumpkin
100 grams sweet basil leaves
2 tablespoons white peppercorns
100 grams red shallots
½ tablespoon shrimp paste
2 tablespoons fish sauce
1 teaspoon salt
1 litre water

153

1. Wash the prawns and remove the black line from the spine.
2. Peel the gourd and pumpkin and cut them into bite-sized chunks. Wash and clean the mushrooms and slice in half. Cut the young corn tips into bite-sized pieces. Pick the basil into individual leaves. Peel and slice the shallots for pounding with the shrimp paste.
3. In a mortar, pound the white peppercorns finely, add the shallots and when they are well mixed, add the shrimp paste and pound all three into a fine paste.
4. Place the water in a pan on the stove. Add the pounded shrimp paste. When it has come to a boil, add the pumpkin, baby corn and straw mushrooms. When the pumpkin and baby corn are almost cooked, add the gourd.
5. Season to taste with salt and fish sauce, then add the prawns and the sweet basil leaves. When the prawns are cooked, remove from the heat and serve.

TAMARIND AND FISH SOUP WITH MINI OMELETTES

Kaeng som dok sano chup khai tod

Ingredients

200 grams *sano* flowers (substitute with edible
    flowers such as nasturtiums)
3 eggs
8 tiger prawns
150 grams sea bass flesh
½ cup *kaeng som* curry paste
¼ cup tamarind sauce
3 tablespoons fish sauce
¼ cup palm sugar
2 ½ cups water
100 grams finger root galanga
½ cup vegetable oil

1. Remove the stems from the flowers, wash and set aside. Crack the eggs into a bowl and beat till well mixed. Stir in the *sano* flowers.
2. Heat the oil in a wok and pour in the egg and flower mixture to create an omelette. Flip about 3 times to ensure even cooking, leaving for 1 minute each side. Remove and cut into small triangles.
3. Pour ½ cup of water into a pan and bring to a boil. Add the sea bass and poach until cooked. Remove the fish and keep the water allowing both to cool. Mix fish and broth in a food processor until smooth.
4. Pound the pre-chopped finger root galanga until smooth. Either mix with water [½ cup] and then strain through a sieve reserving the water or whizz in the food processor.
5. Boil the remaining water and add the curry paste, fish sauce, tamarind sauce and palm sugar to taste. Then add the fish paste and finger root galanga water. Bring to a boil for a few minutes; add the tiger prawns and turn off the heat.
6. Place the *sano* omelettes into bowls and pour the sauce over before serving.

154

COCONUT AND GALANGAL SOUP WITH SALMON

Tom kha pla salmon

Ingredients

4 pieces fresh salmon approximately
    100 grams each
50 grams galangal
50 grams lemongrass
3 Kaffir lime leaves
4 bird's eye chillies
50 grams red shallots
2 coriander roots
100 grams straw mushrooms
30 grams spring onions
30 grams coriander
30 grams sawtooth coriander
4 dried finger chillies fried
2 cups stock (see page 40)
2 cups coconut cream
¼ cup freshly squeezed lime juice
¼ cup fish sauce
¼ cup sugar

1. Slice the galangal into thin roundels and finely shred the lemongrass; peel the red shallots, pound to crush and roughly chop. Clean the straw mushrooms and slice in half.
2. Bring the stock to a boil, add the galangal, lemongrass, Kaffir lime leaves, chillies, red shallots, coriander root and straw mushrooms.
3. Season to taste with lime juice, sugar and fish sauce.
4. Add the salmon pieces and simmer till cooked.
5. Add the coconut cream and bring briefly to a boil. Don't let the cream separate.

Spoon into bowls and sprinkle with chopped spring onions, finely chopped coriander, sawtooth coriander and fried dried chilli.

157

SPICY SMOKED DRIED FISH SOUP

Tom klong pla krob

Ingredients

4 crispy fish – *pla salid*
1 head galangal
3 stalks lemongrass
5 Kaffir lime leaves
100 grams red shallots
3 coriander roots
100 grams cherry tomatoes
100 grams straw mushrooms
5 dried chillies fried
2 spring onions
2 coriander plants
1 bunch sawtooth coriander
¼ cup fish sauce
¼ cup tamarind paste
1½ litres water
½ litre cooking oil

1. Wash the *pla salid* to reduce the salt content. Remove the flesh and fry this until crisp, Set aside.
2. Prepare the other ingredients. First, peel the galangal and cut into thin roundels. Lightly crush the lemongrass then slice diagonally, tear the Kaffir lime leaves, peel the shallots and lightly crush before chopping coarsely. Wash and clean the coriander roots, tomatoes and mushrooms, slicing the latter in half. Wash the spring onions, coriander, parsley and chop coarsely for the garnish.
3. Set the water in a pan on the stove and bring to a boil. Meanwhile heat a wok and add the galangal, lemongrass, red onion, coriander root, tomatoes and dried chillies, frying until fragrant.
4. Add these spices to boiling water. Bring back to a boil then lower to medium heat. Add the straw mushrooms and season to taste with fish sauce and tamarind sauce. Once the flavour is to your liking, take off the heat.
5. Spoon into bowls. Add the fried *pla salid*, sprinkle with chopped spring onion, coriander and parsley before serving.

158

POT ROAST BEEF WITH THAI SPICES
Neua tun kreung thed Thai

Ingredients

500 grams beef
30 grams mature galangal
3 coriander roots
20 grams garlic
10 grams black peppercorns
20 grams cinnamon
2 cardamom leaves
10 grams tree basil seeds
10 cardamom seeds
20 grams Chinese star anise
2 spring onions
1 red finger chilli
½ cup oyster sauce
¼ cup white soy sauce
¼ cup sugar
8 cups water

1. Cut the beef into 1 inch cubes, place in a saucepan, add 8 cups of water and place on the stove.
2. Take all the spices including the galangal, coriander root and garlic and wrap in muslin to create a bouquet garni. Add to the stew pot.
3. Season with the oyster sauce, white soy sauce and sugar. Simmer on low to medium heat until the beef is tender and the liquid has reduced by half to around 4 cups. Check to make sure it is not too salty as reducing the liquid too much can lead to saltiness.
4. Finely chop the red finger chilli and finely slice the spring onions lengthwise. Soak in cold water for a few minutes then set aside to dry.
5. Once the beef is tender, remove the bag of spices and strain the liquid through a muslin cloth. Spoon the beef and its sauce into bowls and garnish with the finely sliced chilli and spring onion.

STEAMED SEAFOOD CURRY WITH YOUNG COCONUT

Hor mok talae mapraw on

Ingredients

I young coconut
100 grams *pla krai* fish, filleted
50 grams red curry paste (see page 189)
40 grams squid
4 river prawns
2 mussels
40 grams sea bass
I egg
½ cup coconut cream
50 grams finger root galanga
I tablespoon castor sugar
I teaspoon salt
30 grams Indian mulberry leaves
20 grams Thai basil leaves
2 Kaffir lime leaves finely sliced
I red long finger chilli finely sliced
I bunch coriander plucked into sprigs
3 additional tablespoons coconut cream
2 teaspoons rice flour

1. Trim the coconut in readiness for the *hor mok* curry and use a knife or hack saw to remove the top quarter and make a lid. Saw off the bottom so it stands flat. Clean and wash the coconut.

2. Take the finger root galanga and with a little water [¼ cup] blitz in a food processor then strain and keep the liquid. Wash the squid and cut into bite-sized pieces. Peel and clean the prawns. Remove mussels from shell and cut in half.

3. Place the *pla krai* fillets, egg, red curry paste, coconut cream, strained galangal water, salt and sugar in the food processor and mix well. This is the base for the *hor mok*.

4. Mix the *hor mok* mixture with the mussels, squid, prawns and sea bass fillets. Take the mulberry leaves and sweet basil leaves and line the bottom of the prepared coconut. Then fill up to the brim with the *hor mok* mixture.

5. Place the coconut in a steamer on the stove over a low to medium heat for 20-25 minutes after which it should be cooked through.

6. In a saucepan combine 2 teapoons rice flour with 3 tablespoons coconut cream. Mix well then bring to a boil to ensure the flour is cooked. Place the steamed coconut onto a serving dish and decorate with the warm coconut cream and sprinkle with thinly sliced Kaffir lime leaves, sprigs of coriander and the thin slivers of red chilli.

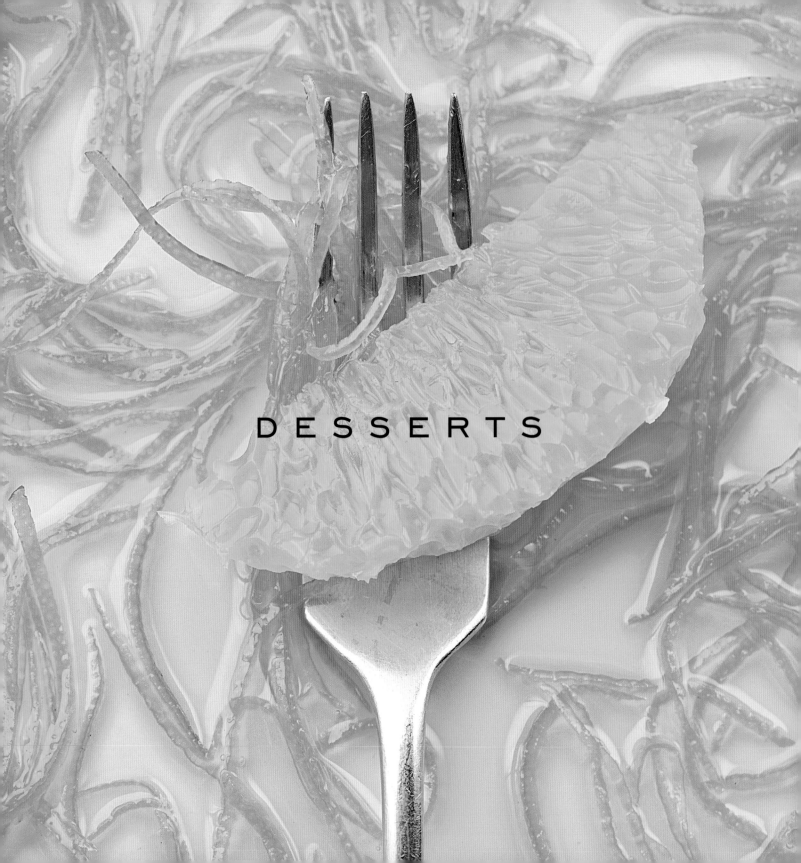

DESSERTS

CARAMELISED BANANAS WITH COCONUT CREAM

Kluai khai cheum rad kati

Ingredients

1 bunch of well-ripened finger bananas
5 cups castor sugar
3 cups water
1 lime
2 pandanus leaves
2 cups coconut cream
3 tablespoons rice flour
½ teaspoon salt

1. Dissolve the sugar in a pan of water and bring to a boil, add the pandanus leaves and squeeze in the lime juice.
2. When the sugar mixture begins to thicken, add the bananas. When they turn golden yellow remove and set aside.
3. Mix the rice flour, coconut cream and salt together. Set on the heat and stir gently, removing when it begins to boil. When serving place the bananas on a dish and pour the coconut cream over.

167

TARO CUSTARD WITH YOUNG COCONUT
Sangkhaya peuk mapraw on

Ingredients
1 green coconut, flesh only
3 duck eggs
½ cup palm sugar
1 cup coconut cream
3 pandanus leaves, finely chopped
1 cup taro, diced into small cubes

1. Mix together the duck eggs, palm sugar, coconut cream and pandanus leaves until the sugar dissolves, then strain through muslin to remove the pandanus leaves. Slice the young coconut flesh.
2. Spoon the mixture into a bowl, add the cubes of taro and young coconut and steam over boiling water for around 25 minutes.
3. Test to see if it is cooked by spearing with a small bamboo stick. If the stick comes out cleanly, the pudding is done.

168

ORANGES IN SYRUP

Som loy keaw

Ingredients

3 Sunkist oranges

350 grams castor sugar

2¼ cups water

1 teaspoon salt

1. Peel the oranges. Set aside the peel and carefully break the oranges into individual segments.
2. Take the orange peel, remove any pith and cut into thin strips preparing enough for approximately ½ cup. Reserve.
3. Take 50 grams of sugar and put in a small pan. Heat until it dissolves and caramelises. Add the sliced orange peel. Add a small amount of water and simmer for a while until the orange peel is cooked. Remove from the heat.
4. Add the remaining sugar to a pan and heat. When the sugar has dissolved add the water. Simmer until it begins to thicken. Add the salt and stir thoroughly then remove from the heat and allow to cool.
5. Place the orange segments in glass serving bowls, add a small amount of the caramelised sliced peel and enough syrup to cover the oranges. Add ice just before serving.

171

CRISPY 'POMEGRANATES' AND ROASTED COCONUT

Tabtim krob mapraw phao

This refreshing dessert is a childhood favourite. Although called pomegranate, it is nothing of the kind and therefore has no seeds that need spitting out. The contrast between the red and white is particularly appealing.

Ingredients

172

I cup water chestnuts, diced
½ cup water
2 cups tapioca flour
3 cups red colouring mixed with water
I cup castor sugar
3 cups coconut cream
3 pandanus leaves
I roasted coconut
I candle for imparting a smokey flavour
  (available from Thai cooking shops)

1. Mix the sugar and pandanus leaves together using your hands to crush the leaves. Add water and bring to a boil. Then strain the liquid and reserve. Pour the coconut cream into a pan, bring to a boil and then remove from the heat.

2. To impart a smokey flavour, use the special culinary candle. [This step is not essential and can be left out if special candle not available] Place the bowls of syrup and coconut cream within a larger receptacle. Light the candle in the middle, blow out and immediately cover with a lid, allowing the smoke to infuse the liquids.

3. Bring a pan of water to a boil and toss in the coated water chestnut dice. When they rise to the top use a slotted spoon to remove them and plunge into iced water. Then spoon into a bowl. When serving in individual bowls, spoon the syrup over the top together with the fresh coconut milk.

4. Split the roasted coconut and cut the flesh into bite-sized pieces, which can be decoratively carved if desired. Place in the bowls with the crispy 'pomegranate'. Add some ice just before serving.

TAPIOCA PUDDING WITH COCONUT CREAM
Tako mun sampalung

TAPIOCA BASE
Ingredients
1 cup freshly grated tapioca
½ cup diced tapioca
2 pandanus leaves
½ cup rice flour
1 cup water
1 cup castor sugar
1 teaspoon salt

1. Boil the diced tapioca until it is cooked (5-10 mins). Reserve.
2. Mix the freshly grated tapioca with the rice flour and water in a pan. Bring to a boil.
3. Season to taste with sugar and salt, continue stirring until the grated tapioca is cooked. Add the diced tapioca and mix well. Check seasoning and remove from the heat.
4. Spoon the tapioca into pre-prepared *krathong* (see page 191) made of pandanus leaf to about ²/₃ full.

CREAM TOPPING
Ingredients
2 cups coconut cream
½ cup rice flour
1 teaspoon salt
2 teaspoons castor sugar

1. In a pan mix together the rice flour, coconut cream and pandanus leaves tied into two knots. Bring to a boil on the stove, stirring continuously. Add the sugar and salt to taste and remove. Take out the two knots of pandanus leaves.
2. Spoon the mixture over the taro base and fill to the top.

175

SWEET COCONUT STEAMED DUMPLINGS
Khanom sai sai

This delicious dessert is slightly more complicated than it appears. The inner stuffing of coconut and palm sugar is enclosed by an outer layer of rice flour pastry before being dipped in the thick coconut cream surround.

176

FILLING
Ingredients
1 cup sticky rice flour
Water steeped with ¼ cup *anchan*
    (butterfly pea) flowers
2 cups grated coconut
1 cup palm sugar
½ teaspoon salt

COCONUT CREAM SURROUND
Ingredients
¼ cup rice flour
1 teaspoon salt
¼ cup sugar

1. To prepare the stuffing, mix the grated coconut with the palm sugar and heat in a pan until sticky. Set aside to cool and fumigate with candle smoke to enhance the flavour (see page 194).
2. To make the rice flour surround, sprinkle some anchan-infused water onto the flour to moisten. Knead the pastry into small balls, roll out and place the prepared filling in the middle and press together to enclose.
3. Simmer the balls until they float to the surface. Remove with a slotted spoon and allow to cool.
4. For the outermost layer of coconut cream, mix the rice flour and coconut cream together and add salt and sugar. Heat the mixture until cooked for roughly 3 minutes and remove from the heat.
5. Add the coconut balls to the cream and ensure each one is well coated. Scoop out one ball at a time making sure a lot of the cream surrounds it. Place into the prepared banana leaf (see page 191). Place the packages into a steamer and cook for about 10 minutes. Allow to cool before serving.

STICKY RICE WITH COCONUT CREAM
Khao neaw moon

STICKY RICE
Ingredients
½ kilogram sticky rice
2 cups coconut cream
1 teaspoon salt
1 cup castor sugar

CARAMEL TOPPING
Ingredients
3 duck eggs
½ cup palm sugar
1 cup coconut cream
3 pandanus leaves, finely chopped

1. Mix together the eggs, palm sugar, coconut cream and pandanus leaves, stirring vigorously until the sugar is dissolved. Then seive through muslin and discard the pandanus leaves.
2. Spoon the strained liquid into a bowl and steam for around 25 minutes. Remove from the steamer and serve with the sticky rice.

COCONUT CREAM TOPPING
Ingredients
1 cup coconut cream
1 tablespoon rice flour
½ teaspoon salt
2 tablespoons sugar

1. Soak the sticky rice in water for at least 4 hours and rinse it through 2-3 times. Drain the water and steam in a receptacle which has been spread with a muslin cloth for 25-30 minutes until cooked.
2. Take the cooked rice while still hot and pour into a saucepan. Add the coconut cream, sugar and salt, stirring until all are well mixed. Close the lid and leave to steep for 30 minutes to an hour.
3. To make the coconut topping, take the coconut cream, salt and sugar, mix well and add the flour. Stir thoroughly then set the mixture on the stove. Remove the pan immediately when it comes to a boil as the coconut cream must not be allowed to separate. When serving arrrange the sticky rice on a plate and top with the thickened coconut cream.

179

APPENDICES

GALANGAL

RED LONG CHILLIES

BIRD'S EYE CHILLIES

PALM SUGAR

RED SHALLOTS

SALTED EGG

GARLIC

HEN'S EGG

SALTED FISH

DRIED LONG CHILLIES

RAW SALTED EGGS

CORIANDER PLANT
INCLUDING ROOT

KAFFIR LIME
LEAVES

LIME

KAFFIR LIME FRUIT

TAMARIND PODS

SALT

INGREDIENTS

TAMARIND
PASTE

FINGER ROOT
GALANGAL

COCONUT

GREEN
PEPPERCORNS

TURMERIC

LEMONGRASS

CASTOR SUGAR

CINNAMON

PRAWN PASTE

PEANUTS

CHINESE
STAR ANISE

ROASTED
CHILLI IN OIL

BLACK PEPPERCORNS

PICKLED GARLIC

FENNEL SEEDS

CORIANDER SEEDS

FISH SAUCE

WHITE PEPPERCORNS

GINGER

GLOSSARY

Agar-agar (วุ้น). *Made from seaweed, this is widely used as a setting agent as no refrigeration is required.*

Aubergines/ US. egg plant (มะเขือ). *Various varieties are used in Thai cooking, the most common being the pea aubergines (มะเขือพวง) which are bitter and are used in Thai curries, and the golf-ball sized ones also used in curries and soup. Long aubergines are used in yum makeau yao (long aubergine salad).*

Bale fruit (มะตูม). *These fruits can be boiled to produce a refreshing drink.*

Bamboo shoots (หน่อไม้). *Are used in some Thai curries and an Isaan dish called gaeng naw mai.*

Banana (กล้วย). *There are 28 varieties in Thailand although the common banana is the best known. The small banana Musa paradisiaca 'Champa' is often used for desserts.*

Banana leaves (ใบตอง). *These are used to wrap food prior to steaming or grilling and also for making receptacles for desserts.*

Basil. *Four varieties of basil are used in Thai cooking:*

> **Lemon basil (ใบแมงลัก).** *Small green leaves with a lemony scent and peppery. Its seeds are used for desserts.*

> **Holy basil (ใบโหระพา).** *Used for stir-fries and strong curries.*

Thai basil (ใบโหระพา). *This has slightly serrated green leaves on purple stems. It is used in stir-fries, red and green curries, and as a garnish for soups.*

Tree basil Ocimum gratissimum **(ยี่หร่า).** *This woody stemmed plant is a shrub. It has a spicy clove-like fragrance and slightly hairy soft leaves.*

Blue gourami (ปลาสลิด). *This freshwater fish is rarely eaten fresh but is usually dried or cured. It is usually grilled or deep fried to concentrate the flavour.*

Boniato (มันเทศ). *This root vegetable is mainly used in Thai desserts.*

Butterfly pea flowers (ดอกอัญชัน). *These flowers are boiled to produce a red liquid which turns purple when mixed with lime juice.*

Cardamom (ลูกกระวาน). *After saffron, this is the world's most expensive spice. They are the seed pods of a member of the ginger family. Added to some curries.*

Cha-om (ชะอม). *This shrub native to Southeast Asia can grow up to 5 m high. It has a slightly bitter leaf that is eaten raw or fried in an omlette.*

Chillies. *Thailand has numerous varieties, although they were originally introduced by the Portuguese.*

Bird's eye chillies (พริกขี้หนู). *These are very small and very hot. They are red or green and form the basis of green curries and many dips.*

Dried chillies (พริกแห้ง). *These need to be soaked in hot water before use.*

Chilli powder (พริกป่น). *Ground dried chillies.*

Finger chillies (พริกชี้ฟ้า). *These are about 5 cm long and mainly green or red. Hot but not overpowering. They can be deseeded to reduce the hotness.*

Roasted chilli paste (น้ำพริกเผา). *This mixture often used as a dip and added to soups is made from chillies, garlic, shallots and some shrimp paste which is then flavoured with fish sauce, palm sugar and tamarind puree.*

Chinese star anise (โป๊ยกั๊ก). *A dried star-shaped pod of a Chinese native tree. It is one of the components of five-spice powder and is used in long-simmered meat and poultry.*

Cinnamon (อบเชย). *One of the oldest known spices indigenous to Sri Lanka. The spice comes from the bark which is rolled into sticks or sold as a powder.*

Coconut (มะพร้าว). *Coconuts are very important in Thai cuisine. The water of young coconuts is a delicious drink and* the flesh is used in desserts. The flesh of more mature coconuts is used to make coconut cream used in curries and desserts. Fresh coconut cream is most easily made by blending in a food processor with water then squeezed to extract the milk and cream. It should then be strained through muslin. Substitute with canned or Tetra-packed coconut cream which will not be so delicious but is easy and can be stored.

Coriander/US Cilantro (ผักชี). The leaves are used as a garnish for salads and the stems and roots are pounded for curry pastes. Equal parts of coriander root/garlic/black pepper is a mixture used in many dishes. Dry coriander does not subsitute. The seeds are used in curries.

Finger root galanga (กระชาย, Boesenburger rotunda). Used in a few Thai dishes such as kaeng tai pla and khanom chin. Is sometimes also referred to as wild ginger.

Fish sauce (น้ำปลา). This is a key ingredient in Thai cooking made from either raw or dried fish. It is added to many dishes instead of just salt and is used for a dipping sauce. Prik nam pla is usually served with all lunch time dishes and consists of bird's eye chillies and fish sauce.

Flours (แป้ง). Various flours are used in Thai cooking as shown on page 192. Rice flour is ground from short-grain rice and is used for noodles and desserts.

Galangal (ข่า). The root is similar to its close relative ginger but it has a pinkish tinge. It is well-known for its use in tom kha kai (chicken soup with galangal).

Garlic (กระเทียม). This is widely used in Thai cooking. Asian varieties have a stronger flavour than European equivalents and the cloves are smaller. Fried garlic is used as a garnish on some dishes.

Ginger (ขิง). In Thailand there are many varieties of edible gingers which are mainly used in soups or with fish.

Ivy gourd (ตำลึง). The leaves are used in soups and as an accompaniment to phad Thai.

Hydrolysed lime water (น้ำปูนใส). This is made from lime powder and water. It is used to soak vegetables and in some dishes.

Kaffir lime leaves (ใบมะกรูด). These leaves are widely used in Thai cooking, whether whole in soups and curries, or finely sliced in salads. The fruit is also sometimes used.

Lemongrass (ตะไคร้). This grass-like plant has a citrus taste. The white part is chopped or pounded and added to pastes and salads. The whole stem can be added to curries and soups.

Limes (มะนาว). Thai limes are smaller than European limes. The juice is widely used in cooking, in particular yum salads and spicy soups.

Mango (มะม่วง). These are used both when ripe as a delicious dessert with sticky rice and also when green, finely sliced in various yums (Thai salads).

Mint (ใบสะระแหน่). This is used in yums, in particular some Northeastern dishes.

Morning glory (ผักบุ้ง). Generally stir-fried with oyster or soy sauce, this can also be deep fried to make a delicious salad.

Mung beans (ถั่วเหลือง). These are used as the basis for khanom chin and in Thai desserts. They are also used for glass noodles (wun sen).

Noodles. These reflect the Chinese influence on Thai cuisine. See page 196 for a full list of noodles and their use.

Palm sugar (น้ำตาลปีบ). Made from boiled down sap of several kinds of palm tree, including the palmyra palm and the sugar palm of India, palm sugar ranges in colour from pale golden to deep brown.

Pandan leaves (ใบเตย). Are used for wrapping prior to steam and also to impart a delicate sweet flavour.

Papaya (มะละกอ). Eaten as a fruit when ripe, while unripe it forms the main ingredient of the famous somtum salad.

Pepper (พริกไทย). Green peppercorns are used in some Thai dishes such as deep fried crispy catfish. Black peppercorns are an important ingredient in making curry paste.

185

Rice (ข้าว). *Thai long-grained rice is famous throughout the world, in particular* khao hom mali, *jasmine rice. It is eaten as a staple at every meal and, in addition, for many years Thailand topped the table for rice exports. All the rice is the same species,* Oryza sativa, *but over the centuries, many varieties have been bred or evolved. A key division is between the boiled rice eaten in south and central Thailand, and the sticky rice eaten in the North and Northeast.*

Rosella (กระเจี๊ยบ). *The leaves of the rosella shrub are used in soups and curries (sorrel can substitute). The fruits are boiled to produce a beautiful crimson liquid used for drinks.*

Sawtooth coriander (ผักชีฝรั่ง, Eryngium foetidum). *Although native to Mexico and South America, the herb is found worldwide. Used widely in Thai cooking in salads and some soups.*

Snake beans (ถั่วฝักยาว). *These are also known as long beans. They can grow to 15 inches. They are tougher than European green beans and can be knotted into bite-size portions.*

Snake gourd (บวบงู). *This green, ribbed gourd is used in soups and also dipped in* nam prik.

Shallots (หอมแดง). *Shallots may well have originated in Southeast Asia from where they travelled to India and further west. Smaller than their Mediterranean cousins, they grow in bulbs like garlic.*

Shrimp, dried (กุ้งแห้ง). *These are used for salads and sometimes pounded for sauces. Soak for about hour before use.*

Shrimp paste (กะปิ). *This is used both in Thai cooking and as a dipping sauce. It is made from fermented ground shrimp mixed with salt.* Nam prik kapi *is a spicy sauce based on shrimp paste and often eaten with short mackerel and steamed and raw vegetables.*

Straw mushrooms (เห็ดฟาง, Volvariella volvacea). *This is a species of edible mushroom cultivated throughout East and Southeast Asia and used extensively in Asian cuisines.*

Tamarind (มะขาม). *These curving bean-like pods grow on large trees with small leaves. Tamarind gives a sweet/sour flavour to many Thai dishes. Can be bought as concentrate in bottles and as blocks of compressed pulp that needs to be soaked and deseeded.*

Taro root (เผือก). *This is mainly used for making Thai desserts.*

Tindora (แตงกวา). *Thai cucumbers are paler green and longitudinally striped. They are also shorter at only 2-3 inches long.*

Tofu (เต้าหู้). *Also known as bean curd, it is made from an extract of soy beans. The soft, white variety is known as silken tofu and is used in some soups. The firmer variety is cut into cubes or slices and deep fried.*

Turmeric (ขมิ้น). *The turmeric plant is related to ginger and the fresh root is used in some salads and for dipping in sauces. The bright yellow powder is used in many curries.*

Vietnamese coriander (ผักแพรว). *This is used as an accompaniment when serving a dipping sauce.*

Water chestnuts (แห้ว). *These walnut-sized brown bulbs need to be peeled. It is somewhat tasteless but has a crisp texture similar to apples. It is used to make* tuptim krob *(see page 172).*

White Radish:

    fresh (หัวไช้เท้า) *is used in soups.*
    dried (หัวไช้โป๊) *is used in* phad Thai *(see page 55).*

Wild bitter gourd (มะระขี้นก). *The bitter taste can be reduced by rubbing with salt and leaving for a few hours.*

Wild pepper leaves (Piper samentosum, ใบชะพลู). *These are often confused with betel leaves. It is used for the delicious snack of* Miang Kam *(see page 80).*

Winged beans (ถั่วพู). *These crunchy beans are used in winged bean salad and in tod mun fish cakes.*

186

Bai horapa (ใบโหระพา) – Thai basil

Bai kaprao (ใบกระเพา) – holy basil

Bai cha plu (ใบชะพลู) – wide pepper leaves

Bai makrud (ใบมะกรูด) – Kaffir lime leaves

Bai manglak (ใบแมงลัก) – lemon basil

Bai saranae (ใบสะระแหน่) – mint

Bai toey (ใบเตย) – pandanus leaves

Bai tong (ใบตอง) – banana leaves

Buap ngu (บวบงู) – snake gourd

Cha-om (ชะอม) – acacia pennata

Dok anchan (ดอกอัญชัน) – butterfly pea flowers

Het fang (เห็ดฟาง) – straw mushroom

Hua chai po (หัวไชโป้ว) – salted dried radish

Hua chai tao (หัวไชเท้า) – fresh radish

Kapi (กะปิ) – shrimp paste

Kha (ข่า) – galangal

Khao (ข้าว) – rice

Khing (ขิง) – ginger

Kluai (กล้วย) – banana

Krachai (กระชาย) – finger root galangal

Krajieb (กระเจี๊ยบ) – rosella

Kratiem (กระเทียม) – garlic

Kung haeng (กุ้งแห้ง) – dried shrimp

Luk krawan (ลูกกระวาน) – cardamon

Madum (มะตูม) – bale fruit

Makam (มะขาม) – tamarind

Makeua (มะเขือ) – aubergine/eggplant

Malagaw (มะละกอ) – papaya

Mamuang (มะม่วง) – mango

Manaw (มะนาว) – lime

Mapraw (มะพร้าว) – coconut

Mara khi nok (มะระขี้นก) – wide bitter gourd

Mun tet (มันเทศ) – boniato

Nam prik (น้ำพริก) – spicy dipping sauce

Nam prik pao (น้ำพริกเผา) – roasted chillies in oil

Naw mai (หน่อไม้) – bamboo shoots

Ob cheuy (อบเชย) – cinnamon

Paeng (ผึ้ง) – flour

Pak boong (ผักบุ้ง) – water spinach

Pak chi (ผักชี) – coriander

Pla salid (ปลาสลิด) – blue gourami, a freshwater fish

Poei kak (โป๊ยกั๊ก) – Chinese star anise

Prik chi fa (พริกชี้ฟ้า) – finger chillies

Prik haeng (พริกแกง) – dried chillies

Prik khi nu (พริกขี้หนู) – bird's eye chillies

Prik pon (พริกป่น) – chilli powder

Prik Thai (พริกไทย) – pepper

Sen (เส้น) – noodles

Som-o (ส้มโอ) – pomelo

Taeng kwa (แตงกวา) – tindora

Tamlung (ตำลึง) – ivy gourd

Taohu (เต้าหู้) – tofu

Tua fak yao (ถั่วฝักยาว) –snake beans

Tua leung (ถั่วเหลือง) –mung beans

Tua pu (ถั่วพู) –winged beans

Wun (วุ้น)– gelatin-like substance

Yi rha (ยี่หร่า) – tree basil

187

How to: Make A Red Curry Paste

ROASTED
CORIANDER SEEDS

CHOPPED
CORIANDER ROOTS

SLICED GALANGAL

DRIED CHILLI

WHITE PEPPER

CHOPPED KAFFIR
LIME PEEL

SLICED LEMONGRASS

GARLIC

RED BIRD'S
EYE CHILLI

ROASTED CUMIN SEEDS

SALT

SLICED SHALLOT

SHRIMP PASTE

ADD SALT

WHITE PEPPERCORNS

ROASTED CUMIN SEEDS

ROASTED CORIANDER SEEDS

CHOPPED KAFFIR LIME PEEL

CHOPPED CORIANDER ROOTS

SLICED GALANGAL

SLICED LEMONGRASS

POUND THE INGREDIENTS THOROUGHLY

ADD SLICED SHALLOT

GARLIC

RED BIRD'S EYE CHILLI

ADD DRIED CHILLI AND POUND

ADD SHRIMP PASTE AND POUND

CURRY PASTE

Fold the Kaffir Lime Leaves and remove the stems

Roll the leaves together tightly and chop

Chopping Lemongrass

Peel raw mango and slice thinly

Stack the slices together and slice into thin strips

Slicing Galangal

Chopping Red shallots

Chopping Bird's Eye Chilli

Chopping Spring Onions

Materials and Tools

Cut 2 ovals, one slightly smaller

Place smaller oval on larger one with shiny side facing out.

Put the pudding in the centre

Fold both sides of the leaves together

Fold one end in to enclose the puddings

Press in the sides

Hold the top of the parcel

Secure with a small bamboo pin

Adjust the pin nicely

The completed package

How to: Make crispy batter

INGREDIENTS: (L TO R) SALT, EGG, FLOUR, BAKING POWDER, PLAIN FLOUR WATER, SODA WATER

POUR IN THE PLAIN FLOUR

ADD THE RICE FLOUR

ADD BAKING POWDER

SALT

MIX ALL TOGETHER

ADD ONE EGG

ADD SODA AND WATER

USE A WHISK AND BEAT TOGETHER

How to: Make egg net

Set a medium pan on a low heat

Coat the pan thoroughly with oil

Pour egg mixture into an icing sugar funnel

To about half way

Dribble into the pan and make horizontal lines

Make verlical lines to form a grid

Remove as soon as cooked

3-LAYERED STEAMER

BASKET FOR STICKY RICE

TERRACOTTA POT WITH LID
FOR KHAO KRIEB PAK MOR

194

GRANITE PESTLE &
MORTAR FOR
CURRY PASTE

TERRACOTTA
MORTAR FOR
SOM TUM

CANDLE FOR
SMOKY-FLAVOURED
DESSERTS

BRASS WOK

SIEVES

COCONUT SCRAPERS

WOODEN PADDLES

195

CONDIMENTS FOR NOODLES

CHOPPER

LADLES

MOULD FOR COCONUT CUPCAKES

DIFFERENT TYPES OF NOODLES

CHINESE EGG NOODLES

CHANTHABURI NOODLES

FRESH THAI RICE NOODLES

NARROW RICE NOODLES

FLAT CHINESE EGG NOODLES

FERMENTED THAI RICE NOODLES

WHITE NOODLES

VIETNAMESE PASTAS

VERMICELLI

196

INDEX

All the basic ingredients so common to Thai cuisine, such as shallots, garlic, chillies, lemongrass, Kaffir lime, fish sauce, etc, are not indexed, except where they are central to a dish. You can find a list of ingredients and how to use them in the Ingredients (182-83) and Glossary (184-87), as well photographs showing the ingredients being chopped and prepared, together with the equipment you will need.

Do look at our website for our weekly menus so you can see various combinations. We have not listed all the wonderful fruits we serve at the end of the meal as this depends on the season.

198

199